MEDIEVAL KNIGHT
Read Me a Book!

Adrienne Wigdortz Anderson

**The Scarecrow Press, Inc.
Lanham, Md., & London
1999**

03 CYPAR

SCARECROW PRESS, INC.

Published in the United States of America
by Scarecrow Press, Inc.,
4720 Boston Way, Lanham, Maryland 20706

4 Pleydell Gardens, Folkestone
Kent CT20 2DN, England

British Library Cataloguing in Publication Information Available

Library of Congress Cataloging-in-Publication Data

Anderson, Adrienne Wigdortz.
    Medieval knight—read me a book! / Adrienne Wigdortz Anderson.
      p. cm.
    Includes bibliographical references and index.
    ISBN 0-8108-3517-7 (pbk. : alk. paper)
    1. Storytelling—United States. 2. Children's libraries—Activity
programs—United States. 3. Activity programs in education—United
States. 4. History—Study and teaching (Elementary)—United States.
5. Historical reenactments—Study and teaching (Elementary)—United
States. I. Title.
LB1042.A538   1999
372.67′7—dc21   98-29284
                                               CIP

Printed in the United States of America

The paper used in this publication meets the minimum requirements of
American National Standard for Information Sciences—Permanence of
Paper for Printed Library Materials, ANSI Z39.48–1984.

This book is dedicated with love to my husband Steven, my daughter Blair, and my parents, Hortense and Louis Wigdortz.

Many thanks to my mentor Harriette S. Abels for her guidance and to Field Weber, Renay Griser, and the many librarians and children's book specialists at my local book stores who helped me with my research.

Thanks also to all the Guest Readers, teachers, students, and librarians who participated and contributed to the Guest Readers Program.

Adrienne Wigdortz Anderson
Creator of the Guest Readers Program

Contents

Foreword

When I first met Shawn, he was eight and could not read. He had literally conned his way through the first couple grades of school and probably could have gone a lot further with the ruse if I had not come into his life as his new father.

I needed a way to reach him. Reading drills bored him. He simply was not very interested in reading. Television was his love and *The Dukes of Hazzard* was his favorite show. At the time, I was working on that show at CBS. I got an idea. I started bringing home scripts. Each night after dinner, everyone in the family would take parts, and we would read the script aloud. Shawn would usually be Bo. His sister was Luke. His mother was Daisy. And I would be Uncle Jesse, Sheriff Roscoe, and mean old Boss Hogg. Shawn Piller learned to read.

I tell this story for a couple of reasons. One, to explain why a man who creates television shows for a living would have the nerve to write the foreword to a book about reading. And two, as Adrienne Wigdortz Anderson shows in this book, because we must use every creative approach we can find to make reading part of our children's lives.

Reading aloud is such a useful tool in teaching, and the Guest Readers Program is a wonderfully effective aid to schools. This is a way to help our children learn to love learning. Nothing in this life is more dangerous than ignorance, and nothing is more important than education. We must take an active role in the education of our children—our kids need that from us. There are too many stimuli, too many other influences that pull on their attention these days. Teachers cannot do it alone.

Our country needs that from us as well. We can help make this generation the best-educated generation in the history of America if we choose to get involved. The Guest Readers Program is one great way to get started in your community.

I had a great time when I read to the kids. I think I got as much out of it as they did. By then, I was the executive producer of *Star Trek: The Next Generation,* and the children's interest in *Star Trek* reminded me once again that television does not have to be the enemy. I used their interest in television and read them a funny book, *The Bionic Bunny Show* by Marc Brown and Laurene Krasny. In a way, I felt like the captain of a space ship taking them on an exciting and thrilling journey into the unknown.

In truth, that is what happens every time we open a book to read with our children.

—MICHAEL PILLER
creator/creative consultant/executive producer
of *Star Trek: Deep Space Nine* and
Star Trek: Voyager; executive producer of
Star Trek: The Next Generation

Introduction

Police helicopters and squad cars surrounded the elementary school within minutes of receiving a telephone call reporting possible snipers on campus. The caller said two men dressed in army fatigues were unloading assault weapons from their car.

Fortunately, it was all a mistake. The men, Civil War interpreters dressed in blue Union uniforms and carrying muskets, were visiting the school as Guest Readers at my invitation!

As a parent volunteer, I created and organized a Guest Readers Program for a preschool and later introduced the program to elementary and middle schools. Not all the presentations caused as much excitement as the one described above, but all were interesting and informative.

The Guest Readers Program is an innovative way to motivate kids to become avid readers. Guest Readers are recruited from the community to read not "just any story," but instead books related to their jobs or special interests. Discussion or demonstrations usually follow. Thus the world of books becomes more compelling and real than ever before.

The program can be adapted for use in libraries, camps, scouting programs, or any organization that wishes to positively reinforce the idea that reading is a pleasurable experience.

The benefits of the Guest Readers Program are many: It sends a message that both women and men, from all walks of life, like to read. Children discover that reading is not just a "girl thing" or appreciated only by academics.

At the same time, the Guest Readers Program introduces children to a variety of occupations and professions, broadens their view of the world, and enriches their experiences. Most schools find it impractical or financially prohibitive to sponsor frequent field trips. With the Guest Readers Program, the world comes to the classroom.

As a result, the children become more open to exploring new areas of interest and a wider variety of books than they would have chosen on their own. Even school subjects that may seem dry and boring, such as math and history, get a shot of vitality when presented by a Guest Reader.

Imagine the excitement the students felt when a re-enactor of the medieval era read the legend of *Sir Gawain and the Loathly Damsel* by Joanna Troughton and then, with his colleague, participated in a presentation of mock combat with shield and sword. Later, a boy rushed into the library where I was setting up a display of books. I overheard him animatedly report to the librarian, "I just saw ladies and lords and knights in shining armor! I want to know more about the Middle Ages. Do you have any books on the subject?"

Equally important, the Guest Readers Program inspires kids to read. Illiteracy is one of America's leading educational problems and an issue that has become a personal cause of many of our country's leaders, including former First Lady Barbara Bush, 1997 Miss America Tara Holland, and President Bill Clinton.

According to experts, reading aloud to children is a crucial step toward helping them develop into good readers. Reading aloud promotes the enjoyment of the written word while creating a special bond between reader and audience. Children begin to perceive reading as a fun activity. Reading aloud is the cornerstone of the Guest Readers Program.

The children are not the only ones to benefit from the Guest Readers Program. In today's political climate in which people don't want to rely on the government to solve their problems, the Guest Readers Program is a wonderful opportunity for the community to have a positive influence on education. Volunteer readers are delighted to share their talents, expertise, and stories. Additionally, they appreciate the importance of serving as role models.

On a personal level I have found that helping the school by coordinating the Guest Readers Program is gratifying, especially when I realize I have sparked a child's desire to read and learn more about a topic. A case in point is the boy who was "turned on" to medieval history. His enthusiasm was all I needed to know that my efforts were well worth it!

After the Guest Readers Program became known through publicity, many educators, librarians, and parents contacted me for information on how to start the program in their own schools. As a result, I wrote *Firefighter—Read Me a Book!* (Scarecrow Press, 1993, foreword by Los Angeles Mayor Tom Bradley), which is a comprehensive guide for people working with children in preschool to second grade. *Medieval Knight—Read Me a Book!* is the sequel to that and describes how to implement the program in the upper-elementary to middle-school grades.

The first chapter, Getting It Together, explains how to find a Guest Reader and how to select a story to match the Guest Reader's topic. This is followed by specific, detailed program plans. Each program plan includes a suggested Guest Reader; guidelines on how to find the Guest Reader; the title of a read-aloud book (or other appropriate reading materials) and a synopsis of the story line; suggestions for introducing the Guest Reader and book, and ideas for discussion topics and/or demonstrations. Each plan also provides a list of related books, magazines, videos, activities, songs, poems, and games that help develop the theme. Another chapter lists additional ideas for Guest Readers and read-aloud books. Throughout these pages I talk about my experience with the Guest Readers Program. In the last chapter, a few of the Guest Readers, librarians, educators, and students who participated in the program share their thoughts. Finally, the appendix provides sample materials for arranging Guest Reader appearances.

I hope that *Medieval Knight—Read Me a Book!* will help teachers, librarians, counselors, scout leaders, and parents create an exhilarating experience that motivates young people to read. Do not be surprised if your neighborhood banker, high-school track coach, or local television news anchor is just the right person to get your kids "hooked on books"!

Getting It Together

At the end of my daughter's last year of elementary school I attended a luncheon where I received one of the Rotary Club "Service Above Self" Awards. The awards were presented to those individuals who made significant contributions to their schools. I was honored for coordinating the Guest Readers Program at the school my daughter attended.

After the ceremony, the assistant principal of our neighborhood middle school introduced herself and asked me to continue the program there. I was pleased that she was interested, but I was skeptical that it could work with older students. Would adolescents enjoy being "read to," or would they think it babyish?

She assured me that the students would be delighted to hear read-aloud books. The following school year, when I launched the program at the middle school, I discovered that she was right. When my family and I moved to another area, and I introduced the program to my daughter's new middle school, the Guest Readers Program proved to be successful there as well. My worries were unfounded and I came to realize, as reading experts have said all along, that there should be no age limit to reading aloud. In fact, the practice should be a life-long habit.

Unfortunately, adults often stop reading to youngsters once they become independent readers. But it is just as important to read to older children as it is to the younger ones. According to the National

Assessment of Educational Progress, there is a dramatic drop in the number of older kids who say they read for fun every day (*Newsweek* Special Edition, *Education: A Consumer's Handbook,* Fall/Winter 1990, p. 12). There are probably many reasons why this happens, but perhaps by sharing a good story or magazine article with them, we adults could help keep the magic of reading alive and encourage the idea that reading is enjoyable and not just a chore.

Certainly, the students' enthusiastic response to the Guest Readers Program demonstrates that kids of all ages enjoy hearing a "good read."

Over the course of ten years I coordinated the Guest Readers Program in a preschool, elementary school, and two middle schools —always in the capacity of a parent-volunteer. Therefore the information in this book is presented from the perspective of a parent-volunteer within a school setting. However, it can easily be adapted for use by teachers, librarians, school administrators, camp counselors, scout leaders, or anyone else working with young people. The program coordinator need not have a background in education— just a desire to pass on the love of books to the next generation.

For a smoother reading of the text, I refer to the Guest Reader and the child as "he" and the teacher as "she."

AGE RANGE

The Program Plans found in the following chapters are designed for youngsters in upper elementary (third grade to fifth/sixth grade) to middle-school level (sixth/seventh grade to eighth/ninth grades). The Program Plans can be adjusted to meet the needs of younger or older children. (For more detailed plans geared to preschoolers and lower elementary-school students, see *Firefighter—Read Me a Book!*)

FINDING THE GUEST READER

I am frequently asked how I find my Guest Readers. The answer is, I consider everyone I know, meet, hear about, or read about in the local paper as potential Guest Readers! You would be surprised how many relatives, friends, and acquaintances represent a wide range of interests and would be terrific Guest Readers. Don't hesitate to invite your banker, your attorney, or your child's gymnastics coach to fill the role. If they turn you down, ask them to refer you to someone else in their field.

Keep on the lookout for stories about interesting people who are featured in the media. One morning I heard a local inventor being interviewed on my favorite talk-radio show. Luckily, his office number was announced over the air. When I telephoned him, he eagerly agreed to be a Guest Reader. If a telephone number or address is not given in the story, call the newspaper, or radio or television stations and ask if they can provide you with this information.

Invite a celebrity to participate in the Guest Readers Program. It is exciting to have someone "famous" visit the school and, just like celebrity endorsements of brand-name products on commercials, it doesn't hurt to have a well-known person endorse the joys of reading. Don't be shy about asking—many celebrities are genuinely eager to become involved in a good cause.

Of course, the best source for Guest Readers is students' family and friends. These are the people who would be most inclined to help the school. Send a letter home requesting volunteers (see appendix). Ask the teachers for leads; they might know of a parent with an interesting occupation. Make an announcement at a meeting of the school's parent organization, such as the PTA. Hang posters in the school where parents will be most likely to see them. Place an advertisement in the school newsletter (see appendix).

Send an item to the local newspaper because sometimes they list volunteer opportunities. Also, contact the Chamber of Commerce, professional organizations, organizations for retired people, volunteer agencies, colleges and high schools, public relations, or community-affairs departments of corporations and museums for speakers. (See appendix for sample invitations and telephone scripts.) To find the address and telephone number of organizations, try the telephone book or the *Encyclopedia of Associations: An Associations Unlimited Reference* (edited by Christine Maurer and Tara E. Sheets. Detroit, MI: Gale [annually updated]) found in the reference section of the library. In addition, consider asking members of the school staff or their spouses to be Guest Readers.

Choose Guest Readers who represent a variety of areas such as the arts, sports, sciences, and community services. Try to invite a diverse cross-section of the population to be Guest Readers, including disabled people, people belonging to different ethnic groups, senior citizens, and high-school and college students.

If possible, help destroy any stereotypes of what is considered *women's work* and *men's work.* For example, I was astonished to learn that many of the children were surprised that one female Guest Reader was a chemist. They had no idea that a woman could be a scientist!

Consider coordinating the Guest Readers' presentations with holidays or special events. Invite the representative from the county registrar–recorder office to talk about voting during election season. Schedule an environmentalist for Earth Day or Arbor Day; a Guide Dog trainer or interpreter for the deaf for International Day of Disabled Persons; a manners' expert before the winter holiday season so that students will learn how to be on their best behavior when they attend family gatherings. Look up the dates for special celebrations in *Chase's Annual Events* found in the reference section of the library.

Try to link the Guest Readers' presentations with subjects the students are learning in class. History comes alive when interpreters of the Middle Ages or Civil War re-enact those periods! A banker explaining savings and investments makes math more relevant to the students' lives. Tips on how to research a report from a newspaper editor provides interesting and valuable insight on what could otherwise be a tedious assignment. A police detective describing how cases are solved will enrich the literature class's unit on mystery novels. Your state representative adds an interesting dimension to social studies, civics, or lessons on government. Guest Readers can enhance the curriculum and bring a refreshing perspective to lessons.

SELECTING THE READ-ALOUD BOOK

The older the group of students, the more of a challenge it is to find suitable material that is interesting and age-appropriate. Remember, though, that selections do not always have to be books. If you find a poem, a newspaper column, or a magazine article that is relevant and likely that the class would enjoy, use it!

Although they may seem ideal, refrain from using "career books." They are usually too dry to read aloud to a group. Books with interesting plots and narratives that stimulate the children's emotions, thinking, and imagination are best. In addition, try to avoid books that are too long, with many lengthy, descriptive paragraphs.

Do not automatically dismiss picture books because you think they are too juvenile. As Jim Trelease says in his *Read Aloud Handbook,* a good story is a good story, and "beautiful and stirring pictures can move fifteen year olds as well as five year olds."

Be sure that the read-aloud selection does not take longer than ten minutes to read. Time yourself while reading at a normal pace. If the story is too good to give up, yet is too long, consider editing it for the presentation.

To find a read-aloud book or related books:

- Check the library's reference books for ideas, such as *A to Zoo: Subject Access to Children's Picture Books,* 3rd edition (by Carolyn W. Lima and John A. Lima. New York: R.R. Bowker, 1989); *Children's Books in Print: A Subject Index to Children's Books* (New York: R.R. Bowker [continually updated]); *Children's Catalog* (New York: H.W. Wilson Company [continually updated]); *Best Books for Children: Preschool through Grade 6* (edited by John T. Gillespie and Corinne J. Naden. New Providence, NJ: R.R. Bowker, 1994); and *Fantasy Literature for Children and Young Adults: An Annotated Bibliography* (by Ruth Nadelman Lynn. New Providence, NJ: R.R. Bowker, 1995).

- Most libraries' card catalogs or computer systems provide a listing of books by topic.

- The children's librarian and clerks in books stores, especially those specializing in children's books, are happy to offer assistance.

- Check out the internet for information about books. Here are a few websites that may be helpful:

  –http://www.ala.org (see links to library web resources)

  –http://sunsite.berkeley.edu/Libweb/littleusa-pub.html

  –http://www.amazon.com

  –http://www.wlma.org/books/chilya.html

BEFORE THE PRESENTATION

- Before scheduling a Guest Reader, check with the principal and teachers to avoid conflicts with other important events such as assemblies, field trips, and tests. Consult with them as to where the program should be held, such as the library, auditorium, or classroom.

- As a reminder, provide the principal, office staff, and teachers with a schedule of the program at least two weeks in advance. Keep a copy of the schedule for yourself and bring it with you on the day of the Guest Reader's visit (see appendix for sample schedule).

- If visitor parking is not readily available, remember to reserve a parking space for the Guest Reader. This is especially important if a vehicle is to be used in a demonstration.

- Make arrangements in advance with the appropriate school personnel for special equipment such as a video monitor, or if the Guest Reader needs assistance transporting equipment from his car to the meeting room.

- Obtain the principal's permission in writing for any out-of-the-ordinary circumstances, such as bringing historic weaponry onto campus. Provide the Guest Reader with one copy of the permission statement and keep a copy for yourself. Bring this copy with you on the day of the Guest Reader's presentation.

- Make sure the room is set up before the Guest Reader's appearance. Is there a chair for him to use? Is there an empty table on which to place equipment? If another class will be participating, are there additional chairs or a carpet for the students to sit on? Is a bottle of water placed conveniently for the Guest Reader?

- Before the Guest Reader's visit, the teacher may wish to create a bulletin-board display that carries out the theme. It will remind the students of the upcoming program, reinforce educational concepts, and add to the excitement of the special day.

- For the same reasons stated above, you or the school librarian may wish to create a book display that carries out the theme. Place the display in the library or meeting room.

- If the Guest Readers Program is sponsored by the library and is open to the public, prominently display posters publicizing the event. Remember to include the name of the Guest Reader, his title, the date, day of week, time, location, target age group of the audience, and telephone number for additional information. Place flyers promoting the event in the children's/young-adult section and book check-out desk. Publicize the event in your local media: call the newspaper and television and radio stations to ask them how far in advance they need to receive the information and how it should be submitted.

Preparing the Guest Reader

Most Guest Readers do not have experience speaking to large groups of people; therefore, it is imperative to prepare them for their appearance. Furthermore, because Guest Readers are volunteering their time, it is important to eliminate any speculation, surprises, or extra work for them. Try to make their visit run as smoothly and pleasantly as possible.

The Telephone Call

When making your initial telephone contact with the Guest Reader, briefly discuss the details of his presentation (see appendix for a sample telephone script):

- Give a brief description of the Guest Readers Program.
- Determine possible dates and times for the visit. (Discuss the school schedule in advance with the principal and teachers so that you have ready a list of available dates and times when you speak with the Guest Reader.) Do your best to accommodate the Guest Reader's schedule. If more than one class will be involved, explain this to the Guest Reader and ask if the presentation can be repeated. Inform him how long it takes to read the story and then together figure out how long the discussion and demonstration will be. (Keep in mind the attention span of the audience and scheduling limitations.) Determine the approximate length of each presentation and how long the entire visit will be. (After the date and time are set with the Guest Reader, alert the principal and teachers. Have the information written down on the main school schedule. Two weeks before the visit, provide the principal and teachers with a reminder.)
- Discuss with the Guest Reader ideas for discussion and demonstration. Bear in mind that some Guest Readers, such as history re-enactors, may have established presentations that they give to school audiences. If this is true, ask what topics are covered in

their talk and demonstration. (If appropriate, ask the Guest Reader to point out how reading is pertinent to his work.)

- Find out if there are any space requirements or special equipment needed for the demonstration.
- Assure the Guest Reader that you will supply the read-aloud book, and that you will send a copy to him in advance for review. Briefly describe the story. Encourage the Guest Reader to tell the story with enthusiasm—to "ham it up" a bit. (Sometimes, the Guest Reader has ideas for reading material. Ask for input, especially if you are having problems finding a book.)
- If pertinent to the presentation, such as a Civil War re-enactment, request that a uniform be worn.
- Give the Guest Reader the address and telephone number of the school. Tell him where to park. Agree on a meeting place, such as the school lobby. Also, mention that you will escort the Guest Reader to each class.
- Assure him that you will send a confirmation letter with the details. (Remember to obtain a mailing address.) Give the Guest Reader your telephone number in case there are further questions.
- Be sure to telephone the Guest Reader again, several days before his appearance, to verify that the information was received and to confirm the arrangements.

The Confirmation Letter

The confirmation letter (see sample in appendix) is probably the most important way to prepare the Guest Reader. For a professional look, type the letter on the school's letterhead. This letter should convey a warm welcome to the Guest Reader, with an attached form or data sheet that provides all the details concerning the presentation. You may not want to use a form and instead include all the pertinent information in the letter itself. However, I have found that a data sheet is easier to follow and, with personal computers, can easily be changed to fit the specific requirements of each individual Guest Reader. No matter which format you decide to use, try to fit all the information onto one page. Include the following:

- Day of week, date, and time of the presentation, including time of arrival.

- Approximate length of time the Guest Reader will spend at the school.
- Approximate length of time for each presentation.
- Number of classes or groups participating.
- Age range and number of students in each group.
- Title, author, and illustrator of the read-aloud book.
- Reminder to wear uniform and to bring equipment.
- Suggestions for discussion topics and/or demonstration.
- Suggestion for introduction of the read-aloud book.
- The school's address and telephone number.
- Directions to the school.

The Guest Readers appreciate guidelines on how to read to youngsters. Copy the sample "Hints for Reading Aloud" found in the appendix and enclose it with the confirmation letter. Also, if appropriate, include the principal's permission letter for any special circumstances, such as historic weaponry. In addition, don't forget to provide in advance a copy of the read-aloud book to the Guest Reader for review. (On the day of the visit, if there are a few minutes available before the presentation, you may want to go over the technique of how to hold the book so that the audience can see the pictures, or, if there are no pictures, the reader's face!)

THE PRESENTATION

The Presentation Schedule

The length of the presentation depends on your group's age and attention span, the subject matter, demonstration, as well as the school's and Guest Reader's schedules. Approximately thirty minutes to one hour seems to work well in most cases. If the presentation ends earlier than the time allotted, do not try to "artificially" prolong it.

Number of Presentations

When I coordinated the Guest Readers Program for the preschool, the school was small enough for all the students to participate. This arrangement was impossible in the elementary school, which had many more classes. Instead, we targeted one grade. The Guest

Readers Program followed these children as they were promoted each year to the next level. The middle school presented yet another problem, because students change classes and teachers throughout the day.

Discuss with the principal which classes will be involved in the program. The number of times a presentation is given will depend on how many groups participate and the Guest Reader's schedule. Try to limit the presentations to two and the Guest Reader's visit to no more than two hours. In order to involve as many students as possible without adding time to the schedule, combine classes to form one group. However, a grouping should not be so large so as to be overwhelming for the Guest Reader and the audience. Ideally, there should not be more than sixty children in a group. Although it cannot always be worked out, try to keep the environment intimate so that the students can get as much out of the reading as possible. Of course, there may be exceptions without any ill effects. For example, in my experience, the ecologists and the medieval-era interpreters gave their presentations with much success to an auditorium filled with students.

Scheduling the Guest Reader

The number of times a Guest Readers Program is scheduled throughout the school year is determined by many factors, such as how much effort and time you, the Program Coordinator, can devote to the project and how much free time the teachers have available. You may find that the higher the grade level, the less time there is for Guest Readers. Therefore a program may be scheduled as often as once a month or, on the other hand, only twice a semester. This needs to be discussed with the principal and teachers.

Suggested Presentation Format

    I. Program Coordinator introduces the Guest Reader.

    II. The Guest Reader introduces the book.

    III. The Guest Reader reads the book.

    IV. The Guest Reader explains his job (or special interest) and discusses various aspects of his work.

V. The Guest Reader gives the demonstration.

VI. Question-and-answer period.

Coordinator's Responsibilities During the Presentation

- One or two days before, or on the morning of the visit, remind the teachers about the Guest Reader.

- Meet the Guest Reader at the prearranged place, such as the school lobby. Take a few minutes to brief the Guest Reader about the schedule and to go over the reading technique. Introduce the Guest Reader to the school principal.

- Escort the Guest Reader to each classroom. If possible, alert each teacher five minutes before the Guest Reader's arrival so that the class will be prepared. This is especially important if one group of students has to move to another room.

- If a presentation is particularly complicated, you may need to recruit an assistant to help you. For example, if a vehicle demonstration and a reading presentation are given simultaneously you will need to be present at one, while the assistant is present at the other.

- Provide the Guest Reader with a glass and a carafe or small bottle of water for his convenience.

- Introduce the Guest Reader. (Suggested introductions are provided in the Program Plans.)

- With the Guest Reader's consent, take photographs during the presentation. (With permission from the principal you can later create a Guest Readers Program display for the school lobby.)

- Assist the Guest Reader. For example, if the Guest Reader brings an item that needs to be viewed up close, walk the item around the room to each student while the Guest Reader continues to speak.

- If the class is shy, get the ball rolling during the question-and-answer period by asking a few of your own questions.

- Towards the end of the presentation, invite the students to the library to "read more about it." Show them other books that deal with the subject.

AFTER THE PRESENTATION

Thank You

Volunteers should be graciously acknowledged. If your school has a party or ceremony honoring volunteers, ask the principal if the Guest Readers can be invited.

Always write a note of appreciation following the Guest Reader's visit. (See sample in appendix.) It is nice to include students' thank-you notes as well. (Sometimes students have created artwork or stories inspired by the Guest Reader, and these can also be sent.) I know that the Guest Readers enjoy hearing from the students.

It is a good idea to give the teachers a deadline to give you the thank-you notes so that you can mail them all at the same time. Tell the teachers in advance that the notes will be mailed, and therefore the notes, cards, or artwork need to be a specific size in order to fit into a large mailing envelope.

Activities

To reinforce the ideas that the Guest Reader presented and to add a special dimension to the program experience, provide the teachers with a list of related songs, poetry, books, and ideas for follow-up projects. This is explained in the following chapter, Program Plans.

Updates

Several times throughout the school year, send a letter to the parents with an updated list of Guest Readers, the read-aloud books, and the related books. (For interested parents, provide a complete bibliography.) Suggest to them that they encourage their children to do additional reading on the subject. (See appendix, sample update letter to parents.)

Reminders

On the day of the Guest Reader's visit, and for a short period thereafter, prominently display the read-aloud book and related books in the classroom or library. Hopefully this will inspire the students to borrow the books.

Bulletin Board

At the end of each semester or the year, create a school-lobby bulletin-board display of the students' drawings and stories as well as photographs taken of the Guest Readers. It will serve as a reminder of the enriching experiences that the Guest Readers provided.

Introduction to
Program Plans

The Program Plans provide suggestions for Guest Reader presentations. Use whatever is helpful. As stated previously, the Program Plans are geared to students in third to eighth/ninth grades. Adapt the plans to meet the needs and age level of your group.

The Guest Reader's introduction, ideas for discussion topics, and demonstrations are there for you to share with the Guest Reader. In the confirmation letter or when conferring with the Guest Reader over the telephone, stress that these ideas are only suggestions. Because of time limitations, not all discussion topics can be covered. Also, the age of the children is a factor when selecting topics. Therefore the Guest Reader should pick and choose from the list, or he should come up with his own.

The books, poetry, magazines, videos, and songs listed in the bibliography are there for teachers and/or parents to share with the students, as are the ideas in the **KIDS' ACTIVITIES** section. The projects are varied and utilize a cross section of skills, such as math, science, art, speech, and music, to carry out the theme of the Program Plan. Teachers can cull whatever is of interest to them from these follow-up projects and should be able to determine which books, poems, magazines, songs, and activities are appropriate for the class. *It is especially important to preview the videos for suitability, age-appropriateness, violence, and offensive language, before showing them to the students.*

If you wish to find additional resources to develop a theme, ask the librarian to direct you to the appropriate reference book. For example, *The Standard Periodical Directory* or *Ulrich's International Periodicals Directory* provide lists of publications for children and the general audience.

The internet is another source for information and ideas for activities. Websites, such as as the ones listed below, will be of interest to kids, parents and teachers (see also pages 5 and 120):

- http://www.ala.org/parentspage/greatsites
- http://www.yahooligans.com

Please note that in the **RELATED BOOKS** and **POETRY** sections, the asterisks (*) signify good alternative read-alouds in case you are unable to find the one recommended in the Program Plan. If you are unsure if the read-aloud is age-appropriate, ask the librarian and/or teacher for guidance.

The suggested age-level listed with each title in the **RELATED BOOKS** section is a rough guideline. After all, ratings such as these are subjective. Remember also that teens can enjoy picture books just as much as younger children. Conversely, third graders might like to have a higher level book read to them. In addition, reading levels vary and some 13 year olds might be more comfortable with a book written for younger readers. The code is as follows: **PJ**—pre-juvenile (preschool to third grade. These books are usually picture books); **J**—juvenile (third grade to seventh grades); **YA**—young adult (seventh grade and up). A plus sign (**+**) signifies "and up."

A synopsis of each fictional book is provided. The titles listed in the nonfiction/informational book section are for the most part self-explanatory.

Program **I** Plan

GUEST READER

Ecologist.

HOW TO FIND THE GUEST READER

- Look in the yellow pages of the telephone book under Environmental, Conservation, and Ecological Organizations.
- Check the white pages of the telephone book under City, County, or State Government Offices section for a conservation or environmental affairs department. If one is not listed, call City Hall or the main government line and ask them to direct you to the appropriate agency.
- Call the science department of the local university, college, or high school. If they cannot provide you with a speaker, ask for a referral.
- Ask the librarian for assistance.
- Contact national ecology organizations and ask for the address and telephone number of their local chapter. If there is none, they may be able to provide information about other groups. Listed below are two well-known organizations with numerous chapters. Additional environmental groups can be found in the *Encyclopedia of Associations: An Associations Unlimited Reference* found in the reference section of the library.

Sierra Club	National Audubon Society
730 Polk Street	700 Broadway
San Francisco, CA 94109	New York, NY 10003-9562
(415) 776-2211	(212) 979-3000

ESTIMATED TIME

One hour.

READ-ALOUD BOOK

The Giving Tree by Shel Silverstein, illustrated by the author. New York: Harper & Row, 1964.

A deceptively simple story about a tree who selflessly provides "the boy" with branches to play in, shade to cool off under, apples to eat, and wood to build a house and a boat. Like many people, the boy takes all these gifts for granted.

The Guest Reader who visited my school was a representative from the organization, TreePeople. The theme of the presentation was how trees are useful to the earth's environment—a wonderful message that any ecologist can discuss. However, if your Guest Reader wishes to focus on another aspect of ecology, check **RELATED BOOKS** and **POETRY** for another read-aloud.

BEFORE THE VISIT

- Decorate the bulletin board with a cut-out of a tree. Attach real leaves that the students have collected to the paper branches.
- Decorate the room with prints of artworks depicting landscape scenes and nature.
- Reserve any equipment the Guest Reader may need, such as a screen and projector for slides or a video-cassette recorder.

INTRODUCTION OF THE GUEST READER

"What is the environment? The environment is all around us. It's everything we need in order to live. The word *environment* comes from the Old French word "viron," which means circle. Like a circle, everything in the world is connected. Whose job is it to take care of our environment? Our Guest Reader (name) from (organization) will let us know."

GUEST READER'S INTRODUCTION OF THE BOOK

"Do you have a favorite tree? One that you climb or sit under to read a book? Trees are an important part of the environment and contribute a great deal to the world. Unfortunately, some people don't realize just how important trees are—as you will see in this book, *The Giving Tree* by Shel Silverstein."

DISCUSSION TOPICS

Suggest to the Guest Reader to:

- Describe how trees are useful to the world:
  - every tree cleans the atmosphere through the process of photosynthesis by absorbing carbon dioxide and releasing oxygen;
  - trees give shade;
  - trees provide shelter and food to birds and animals;
  - tree branches act as windbreaks. Tree roots hold water in the ground and help hold the soil in place so rains do not wash the soil away;
  - decaying leaves and dead trees decompose and help make the soil fertile;
  - people use parts of trees to make foods, medicines, dyes, wood, and paper;
  - trees are beautiful.
- Explain what happens to the environment if trees are cut down (deforestation), including how it could affect the weather patterns and the air quality; how animals and plants could become extinct; how soil could erode; how seeds to grow more trees would disappear; and how beautiful scenery would vanish.
- Explain that nature gives to us, and we must give back to nature. Discuss ways to help the environment, such as recycling.
- Describe the things trees need in order to grow: space, water, and sun.

- Show different types of seeds and discuss how seeds travel, such as via the wind, birds, and animals.

DEMONSTRATION

- Show slides or a video of different types of trees, the effect of pollution on living things, and the effect of deforestation.
- Ask students to "act out" the life of a tree. Roles: the trunk (the child "makes a muscle" with his arms because the trunk must be strong); leaves (the children stand behind the "trunk" and hold arms up as if they are branches with leaves attached. Their fingers open and close to signify the leaves taking in sunlight and carbon dioxide); falling leaves (the children stand behind the branches and fall to the ground and moan "ohhh!" while swaying their arms); roots (the children lay at the bottom of the trunk, saying "slurp, slurp, gurgle, gurgle" to signify that they are absorbing water); crawling animals, such as worms and caterpillars finding sustenance in the dead leaves that fell to the ground; clouds (children move about with fingers opening and closing to signify rain); forest animals, such as birds, squirrels, and bees. While creating this tableau with children from the audience, explain what is going on with the tree. (This demonstration works very well with elementary school-aged children. If there is no time during the Guest Reader's visit consider doing this later, as a follow-up activity.)
- Show how to plant and care for a tree.

KIDS' ACTIVITIES

Ask the students to:

- Define terms such as ecology, acid rain, biodegradable, global warming, ozone layer, habitat, and pollution. Create word games such as word jumbles using these terms.
- Organize an ecology quiz game. Remember to ask questions incorporating ecology terms. Give a prize to the team that wins.
- Review the four environmental "R's":

  Recycle—process of turning used things into new materials

  Reuse—using materials over and over before recycling. For example, wrapping gifts in the comic pages instead of wrapping paper

Reduce—using the smallest of packaging or using less energy. For example, turning off lights that are not being used

Refuse—not using or buying items excessively packaged or made of materials that cannot be recycled. Whenever possible, refuse to use packaging at all. For example, tell the sales clerk that a bag is not needed for a small item. Remember to get the receipt!

- List ways in which the students will follow the four "R's," and additional ways to help preserve the environment. Have them choose at least five eco-friendly actions and write contracts promising to follow them.

- Keep a "green" diary that reviews their own daily actions that affect the environment; note any news about the environment that may appear in the media and record any information about ecology that they learn.

- Each day, collect their personal trash in a bag and weigh it. Remember to use the same type of bag for each day's collection. Compare the amount from day to day. How much more or less garbage did they use? Track the pattern on a graph. Share the results with classmates and record the information in their "green" diaries.

- Cut out a current event about the environment from a newspaper or magazine (or jot down notes when listening to a radio or television newscast). Discuss the items with classmates and retain the clippings in their "green" diaries.

- Discuss and debate environmental issues such as the timber industry versus environmentalists. Remember to include information about New Forestry (where trees are selectively cut, as opposed to clear-cutting). Check out books such as *Earthwise at School* by Linda Lowery and Marybeth Lorbiecki; *The Kids' Earth Handbook* by Sandra Markle; and *Our Endangered Earth: What We Can Do to Save It* by John Langone for information on this topic. See *The Environment: Distinguishing Between Fact and Opinion* by William Dudley for additional issues to debate.

- Read biographies of prominent environmentalists such as John Muir (founder of the Sierra Club); Theodore Roosevelt (U.S. president who doubled the number of national parks and created wildlife refuges); Gaylord Nelson (Wisconsin senator who created

Earth Day); Marjory Stoneman Douglas (champion of the Everglades); Chico Mendes of Brazil (defender of rainforests); and Rachel Carson (author). Write a report or story about one of these people, or create the persona of one of these environmentalists (dress in costume, etc.) and narrate his/her story in the first person as a presentation to the class.

- Read about kids who made a difference such as Andy Lipkis, who as a teenager organized the TreePeople. Books such as *Kid Heros of the Environment* by the EarthWorks Group; *A Kid's Guide to How to Save the Planet* by Billy Goodman; *Save the Earth: An Action Handbook for Kids* by Betty Miles; and *Taking Care of the Earth: Kids in Action* by Laurence Pringle tell the stories of kid activists. Then organize friends and classmates to work on an environmental project affecting the community or the world.

- Write to local, state, or federal government agencies such as the U.S. Department of Agriculture (U.S. Forest Service); U.S. Department of Energy; or the U.S. Environmental Protection Agency. Ask them for educational materials and project ideas.

- Write to environmental action groups and ask them how to become involved in improving the environment. Renew America is a national organization that publishes the *Environmental Success Index,* a list of outstanding local programs in the United States, including projects organized by young people. Also, its Searching For Success awards program recognizes positive environmental projects. Kids For A Clean Environment maintains a speakers bureau and provides information on educational programs. The addresses of these two groups appear below. Find additional listings of environmental organizations in the *Encyclopedia of Associations* or in many of the books mentioned in **RELATED BOOKS**.

Renew America
1400 Sixteenth Street NW,
Suite 710
Washington, DC 20036
(202) 232-2252

Kids For A Clean Environment
P.O. Box 158254
Nashville, TN 37215
(615) 331-7381

- Join an environmental group.
- Write to elected officials in support of environmental laws.

- Organize litter-patrol squads to clean the school playground or halls. Reward the squad that picks up the most litter. (Weigh the returned trash bags.)

- Inspect the packaging of products, including supermarket items, toys, and compact disks. Which brands use too much packaging? Which uses the least? Give a presentation to the class. Write letters of complaint to those companies who overpackage, and complimentary letters to those companies making an effort to reduce packaging.

- Survey local restaurants. Do they recycle? Do they buy beef raised on cleared rainforest lands? What kind of packaging do they use for "take out"? Compare restaurants and plot the information on a graph. Write complimentary letters, promote, and urge their families to patronize those restaurants that are eco-friendly.

- When watching television and films, note how they deal with ecological issues. For example, do the characters drink from mugs or foam cups? Do they recycle? Write down findings and discuss in class. Write complimentary letters to the shows that best portray sensitivity to ecological issues.

- Discuss careers in environmental science such as water-quality engineer, environmental lawyer, environmental activist, hazardous-materials specialist, forester, etc. Find out more about these careers by reading books such as *Careers Inside the World of Environmental Science* by Robert Gartner, and *Save the Earth: An Action Handbook for Kids* by Betty Miles. Interview someone in the field. Ask them to describe their job. What do they like and dislike about it? What is their background? How did they prepare for, and how did they attain their position? Report such findings to classmates.

- Write a story, poem, Haiku, or play about nature or an environmental issue. Illustrate work.

- Draw a picture about something they enjoy in nature or what the environment looks like when polluted. Variation: Draw one scene, two depictions: what it looks like before and after pollution.

- Think about a special "spot" in a natural surrounding where each student retreats for peace and meditation or goes to have fun. Write a description of this haven. Draw a picture of it or take photographs of the spot and create a display explaining why it is special. Variation: Create a video with narration.

- Go on a nature walk. Observe the scenery and write a word-picture describing the natural surroundings. Perform experiments to see if the water is polluted. Take personal heart rates before and after the walk, or before and after walking up a hill. Was the hike aerobic exercise?

- Write a report about the polluted areas in the community. Take photographs of the scenes to accompany the report or create a video documentary.

- Write a report or story about an endangered animal.

- Create a mobile that provides information about endangered animals. Adhere pictures and facts about these animals onto cardboard pieces that are cut into varied shapes like squares, rectangles, or triangles. Use both sides of the cardboard. Punch a small hole in the top of the cardboard. Pull string or yarn through the hole. (Be sure the strings are of different lengths.) Tie the strings onto a wire hanger.

- Make a deck of cards that describes endangered animals and animals found in the rainforest. Choose twenty-six different animals. Cut poster board into fifty-two rectangles the size of playing cards. Place a picture and facts about each animal on twenty-six cards. Photocopy the pictures and facts and adhere onto the remaining twenty-six cards so that there is a pair of cards for each animal. Play Go Fish or Old Maid with these cards. (For Old Maid you will need an extra card. Think of a slogan such as "Don't Pollute" or a picture that you can place on the extra card.)

Projects About Trees

- Plant a tree. Read books such as *Taking Care of the Earth: Kids in Action* by Laurence Pringle for directions. Also, contact a local nursery for advice, or the following organizations for information on this and other activities:

TreePeople
12601 Mulholland Drive
Beverly Hills, CA 90210
(818) 753-4600

Trees for Life
3006 Saint Louis Street
Wichita, KS 67203-5129
(316) 263-7294

- Act out *The Giving Tree* by Shel Silverstein. Choose children to portray "the Boy," "the Tree," and the narrator. Three new actors can be chosen for each scene.

- Present a performance incorporating storytelling, puppet plays, poems, and songs celebrating trees or commenting on ecological issues. The performance can tie in with Arbor Day or Earth Day. If tickets are sold, contribute the money to an ecological cause.

- Create greeting cards commemorating Arbor Day or Earth Day. Use recycled paper! (See *Firefighter—Read Me a Book!* [Scarecrow Press] for a recipe for recycled paper.) Also in celebration of Arbor Day and Earth Day, draw pictures with environmental messages on grocery bags to be used by supermarket employees when packing customers' groceries. (Teachers need to ask local supermarkets to sponsor this activity.) For more arts-and-crafts ideas to mark Earth Day, read *The Best Holiday Crafts Ever!* by Katy Ross, art by Sharon Lane Holm (Brookfield, CT: Millbrook Press, 1997). Contact the following organizations for additional ideas on how to celebrate these special days:

  National Arbor Day   Earth Day USA
    Foundation   Box 470
  100 Arbor Avenue   Petersborough, NH 03458
  Nebraska City, NE 68410   (603) 924-7720
  (402) 474-5655

  Earth Day Resources
  116 New Montgomery, No. 530
  San Francisco, CA 94105
  (415) 495-5987

- Create personal stationery by gluing pressed flowers or leaves on the paper or by decorating the paper with leaf or bark rubbings.

- Create a "nature" collage using twigs, leaves, seeds, and nuts.

- Create a sculpture of a tree by using "junk." Use the cardboard tube in the center of toilet paper or paper towels for the trunk, toothpicks or drinking straws for branches.

- Collect, examine, label, and display different kinds of tree seeds and leaves.

- Take photographs of the variety of trees found in the community. Create a display of the photographs, including information about each type of tree and a map of where the trees are located. Variation: Produce a video.

- Create a poster of a tree. On each leaf write how a tree is useful to the Earth.

- Create a book that gives information about trees, including the process of photosynthesis; a description of the three groupings of forests (boreal, temperate, and tropical rainforests); an explanation of how a person can tell how old a tree is by the number of rings on a tree stump. Or choose one topic about trees to focus on. Here are a few ideas:

–animals that use trees as food and shelter;

–forest products, including nuts; fruit; maple syrup; resins, used to make turpentine; wood to build houses and furniture; wood for fuel; paper products; and medicine;

–contributions of the rainforest to the environment and the effects the disappearance of the rainforest can have on the world. Include interesting facts about the rainforest, such as:

  although rainforests cover only about one-twentieth of the earth's surface, they are home to more than half of all types of plants and animals

  the treetops in a rainforest are called a *canopy,* and the bottom is called the *understory*

  the tallest trees in tropical rainforests are about 165 feet high

  tropical rainforests have an annual rainfall of at least 100 inches. Although rainforests need a lot of rain to grow, they also create rain. Rainforests affect the climate throughout the world

  rainforest plants are estimated to be the source of ingredients used in 25 percent of the drugs doctors prescribe in the United States, including medicines for cancer, high-blood pressure, arthritis, and infections

  the rosy periwinkle grows only in one place: the rainforest of Madagascar. The drug produced from it helps people recover from leukemia

  other rainforest products include: chocolate, bananas, guavas, oranges, papayas, mangoes, cinnamon, paprika, black pepper, rice, rubber, yams, and chicle for chewing gum

it is estimated that 125 acres of tropical rainforests are destroyed every minute—an area equal to almost 100 football fields.

find information about rainforests in books such as *Life in the Rain Forests* by Lucy Baker, photographs from various sources (Chicago: World Book/Two-can, 1997); *The Rain Forest* by Billy Goodman, photographs from various sources (New York: Friedman Publishing, 1991); *Tropical Rainforests* by Jean Hamilton, photographs by many photographers (Parsippany, NJ: Silver Burdett Press, 1995); and *Rain Forest* by Barbara Taylor, photographs by Frank Greenaway (New York: Dorling Kindersley, 1992). See **RELATED BOOKS** for additional sources.

–amazing facts about trees. Listed below are a few culled from the books found in **RELATED BOOKS**:

you can make approximately seven-hundred grocery bags out of a fifteen-year-old tree. In a big supermarket, the clerks would use that number in less than an hour

Americans use 50 million tons of paper every year. To make all that paper, we use more than a *billion* trees

every ton of recycled paper saves 7,000 gallons of water that would be used in paper production

the amount of wood and paper we throw away each year is enough to heat 50 million homes for twenty years

if every American recycled just one-tenth of their newspapers, we would save approximately 25 million trees a year

the most massive living thing on earth is the tree named "General Sherman" in the Sequoia National Park, California. The tree weighs approximately 6,720 tons.

coast redwoods are the tallest trees in the world, but have one of the smallest seeds. (Information from the Treepeople)

- Create a diorama of a rainforest.
- Write a story/report about animals in the rainforest.
- For more information about how to save the rainforests contact:

Rainforest Action Network	Rainforest Alliance
450 Sansome St, Suite 700	650 Bleecker Street
San Francisco, CA 94111	New York, NY 10012
(415) 398-4404	(212) 677-1900

- Create a class poster of trees using hand prints. With a small paintbrush, apply green watercolor paint on the palm and fingers of one hand. Each child then presses down on the white paper. Remember to spread out the fingers so that they look like branches. The green hand-prints are the leaves of the trees. Wash the brush. Apply brown paint onto the brush and with one broad stroke paint the trunk to the bottom of the green hand-prints. Label each hand-print tree with the child's name. Optional: Decorate the green leaves by adhering small pieces of pink tissue paper and small kernels of popcorn. Now the hand prints look like trees with cherry blossoms! Make the popcorn in advance. Eat whatever is left over!

- Create a family tree by drawing a tree with many branches. The branches on one side of the tree should be labeled with maternal grandparents' names and the mother's name. The other side of the tree should represent the father's side of the family. Siblings' names can be written on the trunk of the tree. Optional: Add more branches for more members of the family. Be as elaborate as they desire. Variation: Create a personal poster of hand-print trees representing members of the family. For more information about this subject, read *Do People Grow on Trees? Genealogy for Kids and Other Beginners* by Ira Wolfman, illustrated by Michael Klein (New York: Workman, 1991).

- Eat foods that come from trees such as fruit, nuts, and chocolate.

- Decorate or paint flower pots.

Experiments to Learn About Trees

Experiment I (Polluted Water)

Trees and all living things need water to survive. What happens when the water is polluted?

You need:

- a glass or jar filled with about one inch of water
- a white flower such as a carnation or a rose (or a stalk of celery with leaves)
- food coloring (red works best)

Directions:

- trim the bottom of the flower stem (or celery stalk)
- put a few drops of food coloring into the water
- place the flower (or celery) into the water
- let the flower (or celery) stand in the water for a few hours

Result:

The flower (or celery) has absorbed the colored water. If the water system is polluted, trees, plants, animals, and people will ingest polluted water in the same way.

Experiment II (Acid Rain)

Car exhaust and smoke from power stations and factories pollute the air, causing the rain to become acidic. This is called *acid rain.* (Snow, sleet, hail, and fog can also become polluted.) Winds can blow pollution hundreds of miles from its source before dropping the acid rain. How does acid rain affect living things?

You need:

- two potted houseplants that are the same type. (Obtain permission to use the plants because they may not survive the experiment!)
- four labels or pieces of masking tape
- marking pen
- measuring cup (one-quarter cup)
- lemon juice or vinegar
- watering can or jar

Directions:

- mark two labels "acid." Adhere one label to the pot of one plant, and the other label to the watering can/jar
- mix one-quarter cup lemon juice or vinegar to the water in the watering can/jar labeled "acid."

- mark two labels "water." Adhere one label to the pot of the second plant, and the other label to the second watering can/jar
- fill the watering can/jar marked "water" just with water
- place the two plants side by side so that they receive the same amount of sunlight. Every time the plants need watering (about every two days), give them the same amount with the mixture from the jar that corresponds with its label

Result:

Most likely the plant watered with the solution made with lemon juice or vinegar, both of which are acidic, will not fare as well as the plant nurtured with plain water. This shows how acid rain adversely affects trees, fish, animals, and all living things.

Experiment III (Recycling Rain)

Trees have an effect on the earth's climate.

You need:
- a potted tree seedling (or a green plant)
- large plastic bag
- string

Directions:
- water the tree seedling (or plant).
- place the large plastic bag over the tree and pot, but be careful that the top of the bag is not touching the tree
- tightly tie the string around the pot to keep the plastic bag in place
- place the tree in the sun

Result:

You will notice that droplets of water collect on the inner surface of the bag. Moisture evaporates through the tree's leaves. On a warm day, gallons of water may be released into the air from a single large tree. Imagine how much an entire forest can produce!

Variation: Tie a plastic bag around a leafy end of a branch of an outdoor tree.

For additional projects concerning ecology see *Firefighter—Read Me a Book!* (Program I) and the books listed in **RELATED BOOKS**.

VIDEOS

Instructional Videos

- *The Earth at Risk.* Environmental video series in ten volumes that include: "Acid Rain," "Clean Air," "Clean Water," "Degradation of Land," "Extinction," "Global Warming," "Nuclear Energy," "The Ozone Layer," "The Rainforest," and "Recycling." Hosted by MTV's Kevin Seal. (Schlessinger Video Productions, 1993. 30 minutes for each volume)

- *Help Save Planet Earth.* Hosted by Ted Danson and featuring celebrities such as Whoopi Goldberg and Jamie Lee Curtis. (MCA Universal Home Video, 1990. 71 minutes)

- *Recycle Rex* (Department of Conservation–Disney Educational Productions, n.d., approximately 12 minutes)

Films on Video

- *Captain Planet and the Planeteers: A Hero for Earth* (TBS Productions/DIC Enterprises, Turner Home Entertainment, 1990, 1991. Animated. This episode and the one described below are on one video for a total of 45 minutes. Not Rated)

  Captain Planet and five teenagers, called the "Planeteers," combine their powers to stop the polluter Hoggish Greedly.

  Captain Planet and the Planeteers: Deadly Ransom

  Dr. Blight and Duke Nukem, evil eco-enemies, claim to have stolen enough nuclear waste to poison the entire planet, but it is a ruse to capture Captain Planet.

- *Fern Gully: The Last Rainforest* (FAI Films in association with Youngheart Productions. A Young and Faiman Production Fox Video, 1995. Animated. 76 minutes. Rated G)

A bat named Batty and Cyrsta, a tree fairy, join Pips and the Beetle Boys and Zak, a human, to save the rainforest from sinister Hexxus.

- *Free Willy,* starring Jason James Richter, August Schellenberg, Jayne Atkinson (Warner Brothers/Warner Brothers Home Video, 1993. 112 minutes. Rated PG)

  Willy, an orca, escapes a cruel aquatic zoo.

- *Free Willy 2: The Adventure Home,* starring Jason James Richter, August Schellenberg, Jayne Atkinson (Warner Brothers/Warner Brothers Home Video, 1995. 98 minutes. Rated PG)

  Willy, the orca, does battle with an oil spill.

- *Free Willy 3: The Rescue,* starring Jason James Richter, August Schellenberg, Vincent Berry, Patrick Kilpatrick (Warner Brothers/Warner Brothers Home Video, 1997. 86 minutes. Rated PG)

  Willy, the orca, eludes a boatload of illegal whalers.

- *Once Upon a Forest* (Hanna-Barbera Production/Fox Video, 1993. Animated. 71 minutes. Rated G)

  A wood mouse, mole, and hedgehog find their tranquil lives disrupted when a chemical spill destroys their home, named Dapplewood.

- *Pocahontas* (Walt Disney Productions/Walt Disney Home Video, 1995. Animated. 81 minutes. Rated G)

  The story of the Indian princess who saves John Smith's life also provides a message about caring for the earth.

SONGS

Here is a fun song we all learned in camp that teaches us to be ecologically friendly:

"Be Kind to Your Web-Footed Friends"
(to the tune of "The Stars and Stripes Forever" by John Philip Sousa)

Be kind to your web-footed friends,
For a duck may be somebody's mother,
She lives all alone in a swamp,
Where it is always cold and damp,

You may think that this is the end,
Well, it is!

This can also be found in *The Reader's Digest Children's Songbook,* edited by William L. Simon (Pleasantville, NY: The Reader's Digest Association, 1985), p. 190, and *Rise up Singing: The Group Singing Songbook,* edited by Peter Blood and Anne Patterson, illustrated by Kore Loy McWhirter (Bethlehem, PA: A Sing Out Publication, 1988, 1992), p. 70. Make up new verses, such as "Be Kind to Ole' Mother Earth" or "Be Kind to Big Shady Trees."

Other Songs

- "And the Green Grass Grew All Around . . .," p. 118 in *And the Green Grass Grew All Around: Folk Poetry from Everyone,* compiled by Alvin Schwartz, illustrated by Sue Truesdell (New York: HarperCollins, 1992).

  This can also be found in *The Holiday Song Book,* selected, illustrated, and additional lyrics by Robert Quackenbush (New York: Lothrop, Lee & Shepard, 1977), p. 48 (a different version under the title "Deep in the Woods"), and *Rise up Singing: The Group Singing Songbook,* p. 169.

- "Arbor Day Song" (based on an Israeli folk tune), p. 49 in *The Holiday Song Book.*

- "Colors of the Wind," words by Stephen Schwartz and music by Alan Menken, p. 43 in the book *Pocahontas* (from the animated movie *Pocahontas*). Wonderland Music Company and Walt Disney Music Company. Distributed by Hal Leonard Corp., 1995. (This song has also been recorded.)

- "It's the Same the Whole World Over," p. 50 in *The Holiday Song Book.*

- *John Denver Anthology,* edited by Milton Okun. Port Chester, NY: Cherry Lane Music, 1995. This collection contains many songs about ecology and nature including:

  "American Child," words by Joe Henry and music by John Denver

  "Calypso," words and music by John Denver

  "The Eagle and the Hawk," words by John Denver and music by John Denver and Mike Taylor

"Eclipse," words and music by John Denver

"The Flower that Shattered the Stone," words and music by John Jarvis and Joe Henry

"Garden Song," words and music by David Mallett

"Rocky Mountain High," words by John Denver and music by John Denver and Mike Taylor

"To the Wild County," words and music by John Denver

(These songs have also been recorded.)

- "My Dirty Stream," by Pete Seeger, p. 197 in *Songs That Changed the World,* edited by Wanda Willson Whitman. New York: Crown Publishers, 1969.

- "Pollution," words and music by Tom Lehrer, p. 112 in *Too Many Songs by Tom Lehrer: With Not Enough Drawings by Ronald Searle,* by Tom Lehrer, illustrated by Ronald Searle. New York: Pantheon Books, 1981.

  This song is also found in *Rise up Singing* (see below), p. 37. "Pollution" has been recorded on *That Was the Year That Was* (Reprise Records, 6179-2).

- *Rise up Singing: The Group Singing Songbook,* edited by Peter Blood and Annie Patterson, illustrated by Kore Loy McWhirter. Bethlehem, PA: A Sing Out Publication, 1988, 1992.

  This book has a chapter on ecology songs, pp. 33–39, and outdoor songs, pp. 150–157. Although this book only presents the lyrics of the songs, it provides source listings. You can also buy the *Rise up Singing* teaching tapes, which has the melodies. Check with your local music store.

- "The Turn of the Tide," words and music by Carly Simon and Jacob Brackman, pp. 148 and 170 in *Free to Be . . . a Family,* conceived by Marlo Thomas, illustrated by many artists. New York: Bantam, 1987.

- "On My Pond," words and music by Sarah Durkee and Christopher Cerf, pp. 129 and 168 in *Free to Be . . . a Family*.

- "What Can I Do About Pollution?," words and music by Lois Skiera-Zucek, recorded on *What's in the Sea? Songs About Marine Life and Ocean Ecology*. Long Branch, NJ: Kimbo Records, 1990.

- "Woodman, Spare That Tree," words by George Pope Morris and music by Henry Russell, p. 196 in *Songs That Changed the World.* (See **POETRY**.)

MAGAZINES

- *Audubon Adventures* (newspaper)
  The National Audubon Society
  700 Broadway
  New York, NY 10003-9562
  (212) 979-3000

- *Chicadee* (geared to ages 3–9) or
  Owl Magazine (geared to ages 8–13)
  Young Naturalist Foundation
  500-179 John Street
  Toronto, ON M5T 3G5, Canada
  (416) 340-2700

- *Dolphin Log*
  Cousteau Society
  1933 Cliff Drive, Suite 4
  Santa Barbara, CA 93109-1587
  (213) 656-4422

- *Earth Patrol*
  Earth Matters
  6 Patriot Lane
  Newington, CT 06111-4421
  (no telephone number listed)

- *Kids Face* (newsletter)
  Kids for a Clean Environment
  P.O. Box 158254
  Nashville, TN 37215
  (615) 331-7381

- *Koala Club News*
  Zoological Society of San Diego
  P.O. Box 551
  San Diego, CA 92112-0551
  (619) 231-1515

- *Monkeyshines on Health & Fitness*
  North Carolina Learning Institute for Fitness and Education
  P.O. Box 10245
  Greensboro, NC 27404-0245
  (910) 292-6999

- *Ranger Rick's Nature Magazine*
  Ranger Rick's Nature Club, National Wildlife Federation
  8925 Leesburg Pike
  Vienna, VA 22184-0001
  (703) 790-4000

- *Ranger Rick*–Canada
  Canadian Wildlife Federation
  2740 Queensview Drive
  Ottawa, ON K2B 1A2, Canada
  (613) 721-2286

- *Recycling Stories that Rhyme Newsletter*
  Prosperity & Profits Unlimited
  P.O. Box 416
  Denver, CO 80201-0416
  (303) 575-5676

- *Zoobooks*
  Wildlife Education, Inc.
  9820 Willow Creek Road Ste 300
  San Diego, CA 92131-1112
  (619) 745-0685

POETRY

Poetry Books About Ecology

- * *The A,B,C of the Biosphere,* by Professor Finch, illustrated by Mary Beath. Oracle, AZ: The Biosphere Press, 1993.

- * *Earth Lines: Poems for the Green Age,* illustrated by various artists, photographs from various sources. New York: Greenwillow Books, 1993.

  Choose one or two poems from either of these books for an alternative read-aloud.

Poems About Ecology, the Environment, and Nature

- "All the Smoke," by Eli Siegel, p. 123 in *The Fireside Book of Humorous Poetry,* edited by William Cole, illustrated by various artists. New York: Simon & Schuster, 1959.

- "All Things Bright and Beautiful," by Cecil Frances Alexander, p. 22 in *The Random House Book of Poetry for Children,* selected by Jack Prelutsky, illustrated by Arnold Lobel. New York: Random House, 1983.

- "Auguries of Innocence," by William Blake, p. 22 in *The Random House Book of Poetry for Children.*

- "A Baby Ten Months Old Looks at the Public Domain," by William Stafford, p. 44 in *The New Yorker Book of Poems.* New York: Morrow Quill Paperbacks, 1974.

- "Buffalo Dusk," by Carl Sandburg, p. 58 in *The Random House Book of Poetry for Children.*

  This can also be found in *The Sandburg Treasury: Prose and Poetry for Young People,* by Carl Sandburg, illustrated by Paul Bacon (San Diego: Harcourt Brace Jovanovich, 1970), p. 176; and *Sing a Song of Popcorn: Every Child's Book of Poems,* selected by Beatrice Schenk de Regniers, Eva Moore, Mary Michaels White, and Jan Carr, illustrated by various renowned artists (New York: Scholastic, 1988), p. 81.

- "Cacophony," p. 11 in *Chortles: New and Selected Wordplay Poems,* by Eve Merriam, illustrated by Sheila Hamanaka. New York: Morrow Junior Books, 1981.

- "City, City," by Marci Ridlon, p. 91 in *The Random House Book of Poetry for Children.*

- "Driving to the Beach," by Joanna Cole, p. 217 in *The Random House Book of Poetry for Children.*

- "The Flower-Fed Buffalos," by Vachel Lindsay, p. 25 in *Celebrating America: A Collection of Poems and Images of the American Spirit,* compiled by Laura Whipple, art provided by the Art Institute of Chicago. New York: Philomel Books in association with the Art Institute of Chicago, 1994.

- "Forgive My Guilt," by Robert P. Tristram Coffin, p. 76 in *Reflections on a Gift of Watermelon . . . and Other Modern Verse,* selected by Stephen Dunning, Edward Lueders, and Hugh Smith, photographs from various sources. New York: Lothrop, Lee & Shepard, 1967.

- "Forgotten Language," p. 149 in *Where the Sidewalk Ends,* by Shel Silverstein, illustrated by the author. New York: Harper & Row, 1974.

- "Hurt No Living Thing," by Christina Rossetti, p. 86 in *The Oxford Treasury of Children's Poems,* compiled by Michael Harrison and Christopher Stuart-Clark, illustrated by various artists. Oxford: Oxford University Press, 1988.

  This can also be found in *The Random House Book of Poetry for Children,* p. 72; and *Sing a Song of Popcorn: Every Child's Book of Poems,* p. 78.

- "I Thank You God . . .," by e. e. cummings, p. 146 in *A New Treasury of Poetry,* compiled by Neil Philip, illustrated by John Lawrence. New York: Stewart, Tabori & Chang, 1990.

- "I Won't Hatch," p. 127 in *Where the Sidewalk Ends.*

- "Junk," in *A Poem for a Pickle: Funnybone Verses,* by Eve Merriam, illustrated by Sheila Hamanaka. New York: Morrow Junior Books, 1989.

- "Kindness to Animals," anonymous, p. 49 in *Who Has Seen the Wind?: An Illustrated Collection of Poetry for Young People,* edited by Kathryn Sky-Peck, art provided by the Museum of Fine Arts, Boston. New York: Rizzoli International Publications, and Boston: Museum of Fine Arts, 1991.

- "Leisure," by W. H. Davies, p. 142 in *A New Treasury of Poetry.*

- "Little Things," by James Stephens, p. 41 in *The Arbuthnot Anthology of Children's Literature* (4th ed., rev.), selected by May Hill Arbuthnot, Dorothy M. Broderick, Shelton L. Root, Jr., Mark Taylor, and Evelyn L. Wenzel, illustrated by various artists. New York: Lothrop, Lee & Shepard, 1976.

  This can also be found in *The Random House Book of Poetry for Children,* p.69.

- "My Land Is Fair for Any Eyes to See," by Jesse Stuart, p. 143 in *The Arbuthnot Anthology of Children's Literature* (4th ed., rev.).

- "Nature Is," by Jack Prelutsky, p. 21 in *The Random House Book of Poetry for Children.*

- "Parking Lot Full," p. 10 in *Chortles: New and Selected Wordplay Poems.*

- "Quest,"in *Fresh Paint: New Poems,* by Eve Merriam, illustrated by David Frampton. New York: Macmillan, 1986.

- "Rudolph Is Tired of the City," by Gwendolyn Brooks, p. 92 in *The Random House Book of Poetry for Children.*

•* "Smog," p. 25 in *Sky Songs,* by Myra Cohn Livingston, illustrated by Leonard Everett Fisher. New York: Holiday House, 1984.

•* "Smoke Animals," by Rowena Bastin Bennett, p. 42 in *Celebrating America: A Collection of Poems and Images of the American Spirit.*

- "The Smoking Yokadokas," p. 134 in *Something Big Has Been Here,* by Jack Prelutsky, illustrated by James Stevenson. New York: Greenwillow, 1990.

- "A Thing of Beauty," by John Keats, p. 143 in *A New Treasury of Poetry.*

- "Transcontinent," by Donald Hall, p. 41 in *Reflections on a Gift of Watermelon . . . and Other Modern Verse.*

- "Turning Off the Faucet," p. 86 in *The Butterfly Jar,* by Jeff Moss, illustrated by Chris Demarest. New York: Bantam, 1989.

  This can also be found in *Kids Pick the Funniest Poems,* edited by Bruce Lansky, illustrated by Steve Carpenter. New York: Meadowbrook Press, 1991, p.101.

- "Urban Rainbow," in *A Poem for a Pickle: Funnybone Verses.*

- "The Way of Living Things," by Jack Prelutsky, p. 71 in *The Random House Book of Poetry for Children.*

- "Where the Sidewalk Ends," p. 64 in *Where the Sidewalk Ends.*

- "Who Am I?," by Felice Holman, p. 29 in *My Song Is Beautiful,* selected by Mary Ann Hoberman, illustrated by various artists. Boston: Little, Brown, 1994.

Poetry About Trees

- "Birch Trees," by John Richard Moreland, p. 25 in *The Random House Book of Poetry for Children*.

- "The Brave Old Oak," by Henry Fothergill Chorley, p. 462 in *The World's Best Poetry for Children*, vol. I, prepared by the Editorial Board, Roth Publishing, illustrated by Dimitry Schidlovsky. Great Neck, NY: Poetry Anthology Press, 1986.

- "Brooms," by Dorothy Aldis, p. 18 in *Tomie dePaola's Book of Poems*, collected by Tomie dePaola, illustrated by the author. New York: Putnam's, 1988.

- "City Trees," p. 7 in *Edna St. Vincent Millay's Poems: Selected for Young People*, by Edna St. Vincent Millay, illustrated by Ronald Keller. New York: Harper & Row, 1951, 1979.

- "Climbing," by Aileen Fisher, p. 61 in *The Arbuthnot Anthology of Children's Literature* (4th ed., rev.).

- "A Comparison," by John Farrar, p. 20 in *Who Has Seen the Wind?: An Illustrated Collection of Poetry for Young People*.

- "Dad and the Cat and the Tree," by Kit Wright, p. 60 in *The Oxford Treasury of Children's Poems*.

- "Domus Caedet Arborem (The House Will Fell the Tree)," by Charlotte Mew, p. 118 in *A New Treasury of Poetry*.

- "Every Time I Climb a Tree," by David McCord, p. 62 in *The Arbuthnot Anthology of Children's Literature* (4th ed., rev.).
  This can also be found in *The Random House Book of Poetry for Children*, p. 119.

- "Hideout," by Aileen Fisher, p. 25 in *Tomie dePaola's Book of Poems*.

- "I Robbed the Woods," p. 65 in *I'm Nobody! Who are You?: Poems of Emily Dickinson for Young People*, by Emily Dickinson, illustrated by Rex Schneider. Owings Miles, MD: Stemmer House, 1978.

- "Leaves," by Frank Asch, p. 152 in *A New Treasury of Children's Poetry: Old Favorites and New Discoveries*, selected by Joanna

Cole, illustrated by Judith Gwyn Brown. Garden City, NY: Doubleday, 1984.

- "Leaves," by Ted Hughes, p. 66 in *A Third Poetry Book,* compiled by John Foster, illustrated by Allan Curless, Michael McManus, and John Raynes. Oxford: Oxford University Press, 1982.

- "Lizzie and the Apple Tree," by Julie Holder, p. 62 in *A Third Poetry Book.*

- "Loveliest of Trees, the Cherry Now," by A. E. Housman, p. 119 in *A New Treasury of Poetry.*

- "Maple Feast," by Frances Frost, p. 40 in *The Random House Book of Poetry for Children.*

- "Nigel Gline," p. 76 in *Something Big Has Been Here.*

- "The Oak and the Rose," p. 165 in *A Light in the Attic,* by Shel Silverstein, illustrated by the author. New York: Harper & Row, 1981.

- "One Leaf," by Kaye Starbird, p. 114 in *The Arbuthnot Anthology of Children's Literature* (4th ed., rev.).

- "Our Tree," by Marchette Chute, p. 27 in *Sing a Song of Popcorn: Every Child's Book of Poems.*

- "Rain of Leaves," by Aileen Fisher, p. 19 in *Tomie dePaola's Book of Poems.*

- "To the Wayfarer," anonymous, p. 142 in *The Arbuthnot Anthology of Children's Literature* (4th ed., rev.).

- "Trees," by Harry Behn, p. 129 in *The Arbuthnot Anthology of Children's Literature* (4th ed., rev.).

- "Trees," by Sara Coleridge, p. 170 in *The Oxford Book of Children's Verse,* chosen and edited by Iona and Peter Opie. Oxford: Oxford University Press, 1973.

  This can also found in *The Random House Book of Poetry for Children,* p. 24.

- "Trees," by Joyce Kilmer, p. 561 in *The Best Loved Poems of the American People,* selected by Hazel Felleman. New York: Doubleday, 1936.

- "The Tree," p. 66 in *The Butterfly Jar,* by Jeff Moss, illustrated by Chris Demarest. New York: Bantam, 1989.

- "The Trees Are Down," by Charlotte Mew, p. 117 in *A New Treasury of Poetry.*

- "Tree House," by Shel Silverstein, p. 99 in *Sing a Song of Popcorn: Every Child's Book of Poems.*
  This can also be found in *Where the Sidewalk Ends,* p. 79.

- "The Tree House," by Stanley Cook, p. 55 in *A Third Poetry Book.*

- "The Tree in the Garden," by Christine Chaundler, p. 31 in *The Oxford Treasury of Children's Poems.*

- "Up in the Pine," by Nancy Dingman Watson, p. 140 in *The Random House Book of Poetry for Children.*

- "The War Against Trees," by Stanley Kunitz, p. 621 in *The Harper Anthology of Poetry,* by John Frederick Nims. New York: Harper & Row, 1981.

- "What Do We Plant When We Plant a Tree?," by Warren P. Landers, p. 199 in *The Golden Flute: An Anthology of Poetry for Young Children,* selected by Alice Hubbard and Adeline Babbitt. New York: John Day, 1932.

- "Woodman, Spare That Tree," by George Pope Morris, p. 5 in *The World's Best Poetry for Children,* vol. I.

  See **SONGS** to find a musical version of this poem.

  Find additional poems on the environment in the book *The Big Book for Our Planet,* edited by Ann Durell et al., listed in **RELATED BOOKS**.

Poetry and Prose About Johnny Appleseed

- "Ballad of Johnny Appleseed," by Helmer O. Oleson, p. 27 in *The Arbuthnot Anthology of Children's Literature* (4th ed., rev.).

- A description of Johnny Appleseed, pp. 468–470 in "Abe Lincoln Grows Up," found in *The Sandberg Treasury: Prose and Poetry for Young People.*

•* "Johnny Appleseed! Johnny Appleseed!," retold by Marion Vallat Emrich and George Korson, illustrated by Chris Van Allsburg, pp. 274–276 in *From Sea to Shining Sea: A Treasury of American Folklore and Folk Songs,* compiled by Amy L. Cohn, illustrated by many renowned artists. New York: Scholastic, 1993.

•* *Johnny Appleseed,* by Reeve Linbergh, illustrated by Kathy Jakobsen. Boston: Little, Brown, 1990.

A poem book about Johnny Appleseed.

• *Johnny Appleseed: A Tall Tale,* retold and illustrated by Steven Kellogg. New York: Morrow Junior Books, 1988.

FOLK RHYMES AND RIDDLES ABOUT TREES AND NATURE

The following are found in *And the Green Grass Grows All Around: Folk Poetry From Everyone,* compiled by Alvin Schwartz, illustrated by Sue Truesdell. New York: HarperCollins, 1992:

• "When a big tree falls," p. 143
• "Don't worry if your job is small," p. 143
• "It stays all year," p. 89
• "It runs all day, but never walks," p. 89

STORIES AND ESSAY CONCERNING THE ENVIRONMENT AND TREES

• "Baucis and Philemon" (originally found in *The Age of Fable; or Beauties of Mythology,* by Thomas Bulfinch), pp. 436–438 in *The Arbuthnot Anthology of Children's Literature* (4th ed., rev.), selected by May Hill Arbuthnot et al., illustrated by many artists. New York: Lothrop, Lee & Shepard, 1976.

A myth about trees.

• "The Creation," retold by Joseph Bruchac, illustrated by Leo and Diane Dillon, pp. 4–7 in *From Sea to Shining Sea: A Treasury of American Folklore and Folk Songs,* compiled by Amy L. Cohn, illustrated by many renown artists. New York: Scholastic, 1993.

The Iroquois People's description of how the earth was formed.

- "The Living Community: A Venture into Ecology," by S. Carl Hirsch, pp. 895–897 in *The Arbuthnot Anthology of Children's Literature* (4th ed., rev.).

  An essay.

- "The Gods Made Man," by Natalia Belting, p. 24 in *From Sea to Shining Sea: A Treasury of American Folklore and Folk Songs*.

- "Raven Brings Fresh Water," retold by Fran Martin, illustrated by Leo and Diane Dillon, pp. 8–11 in *From Sea to Shining Sea: A Treasury of American Folklore and Folk Songs*.

  Story by indigenous people of the Pacific Northwest.

- "The Stepchild and the Fruit Trees" (originally found in *Singing Tales of Africa*, retold by Adjai Robinson), pp. 329–330 in *The Arbuthnot Anthology of Children's Literature* (4th ed., rev.).

  African folktale.

•* "The Sting," pp. 167–168 in *Paul Harvey's The Rest of the Story*, by Paul Aurandt. Garden City, NY: Doubleday, 1977.

- "Tia Miseria," retold by Olga Loya, illustrated by T. S. Hyman, pp. 202–205 in *From Sea to Shining Sea: A Treasury of American Folklore and Folk Songs*.

  A Puerto Rican-American tale.

Find additional stories about the environment and trees in the books, *The Big Book for Our Planet*, edited by Ann Durell et al.; *Keepers of the Earth: Native American Stories and Environmental Activities for Children*, by Michael J. Caduto and Joseph Bruchac; and *Keepers of Life: Discovering Plants Through Native American Stories and Earth Activities*, by Michael J. Caduto and Joseph Bruchac (see **RELATED BOOKS**).

RELATED BOOKS

Fiction

- Barron, T. A. *The Ancient One*, illustrated by Anthony Bacon Venti. New York: Philomel Books, 1992. **YA**

Helping to protect a redwood forest from loggers, 13-year old Kate travels back five centuries where a long-vanished Indian tribe is fighting to save the same forest.

- Berenstain, Stan, and Jan Berenstain. *The Berenstain Bears Don't Pollute (Anymore)*, illustrated by the authors. New York: Random House, 1991. **PJ**

Concerned about pollution and waste of natural resources, the Bears form an Earthsavers Club.

- Bliss, Corinne Demas. *Matthew's Meadow*, illustrated by Ted Lewin. San Diego: Harcourt Brace Jovanovich, 1992. **J**

A hawk teaches Matthew to appreciate nature.

•* Cherry, Lynne. *The Great Kapok Tree: A Tale of the Amazon Rain Forest*, illustrated by the author. San Diego: Harcourt Brace Jovanovich, 1990. **PJ**

Animals living in a kapok tree in the Brazilian rainforest try to convince a man from cutting down their home.

- Cowcher, Helen. *Rain Forest*, illustrated by the author. New York: Farrar, Straus and Giroux, 1993. **PJ**

The animals in a rainforest sense danger when trees in the forest are cut down.

- Danziger, Paula. *Earth to Matthew*. New York: Delacorte Press, 1991. **J**

When his class studies ecology, Matthew learns that even small changes in the ecosystem can have lasting effects on the environment. He also discovers that small changes in feelings can affect relationships, especially with his friend Jill.

•* Durell, Ann, Jean Craighead George, and Katherine Paterson, eds. *The Big Book for Our Planet* (written and illustrated by notable authors and illustrators). New York: Dutton Children's Books, 1993. **PJ+**

Nearly thirty stories, poems, and nonfiction works discuss environmental problems. (Choose one of the stories or poems as an alternative read-aloud.)

- Ende, Michael. *The Night of Wishes or the Satanarchaeolideal-*

cohellish Notion Potion, translated by Heike Schwarzbauer and Rick Takvorian. New York: Farrar, Straus and Giroux, 1992. **YA**

A sorcerer tries to complete his evil deeds against the environment.

- Evans, Sanford. *Naomi's Geese.* New York: Simon & Schuster, 1993. **J**

  A story told from the perspective of a young girl, Naomi, and a pair of geese she tries to protect from environmental poisoning.

- George, Jean Craighead. *The Fire Bug Connection: An Ecological Mystery.* New York: HarperCollins, 1993. **J**

  When 12-year-old Maggie receives European fire bugs for her birthday, she uses scientific reasoning to determine the cause of their strange death.

- George, Jean Craighead. *The Missing 'Gator of Gumbo Limbo: An Ecological Mystery.* New York: HarperCollins, 1992. **J**

  A sixth-grade girl, one of five homeless people living in the forest in South Florida, learns about the delicate ecological balance of the forest while searching for an alligator slated for official extermination.

- George, Jean Craighead. *The Talking Earth.* New York: Harper-Collins, 1983. **J+**

  Alone in the Everglades to test the legends of her Indian ancestors, Billie Wind learns to listen to the earth's messages.

- George, Jean Craighead. *Who Really Killed Cock Robin?: An Ecological Mystery.* New York: HarperTrophy, 1991. **J**

  An eighth-grade boy tracks down the killer of the town mascot, Cock Robin.

- Gibbons, Gail. *The Seasons of Arnold's Apple Tree,* illustrated by the author. San Diego: Voyager Books/Harcourt Brace, 1984. **PJ**

  As the season passes, a young boy enjoys a variety of activities as a result of his apple tree. The book includes a recipe for apple pie and describes an apple cider press.

- Glaser, Linda. *Tanya's Big Green Dream,* illustrated by Susan McGinnis. New York: Macmillan, 1994. **J**

When Tanya decides to plant a tree for her Earth Day project, she must think of a way to raise money to buy a tree and to find a place to plant it.

- Mahy, Margaret. *The Girl with the Green Ear: Stories About Magic in Nature*, illustrated by Shirley Hughes. New York: Knopf, 1992. **J**

Nine magical stories with ecological themes.

- McHargue, Georgess. *Beastie.* New York: Delacorte Press, 1992. **J**

A group of children, whose parents are on a scientific expedition looking for evidence of a creature living in a Scottish loch, are concerned about the fate of the "monster."

- Morressy, John. *The Drought on Ziax II*, illustrated by Stanley Skardinsky. New York: Walker, 1978. **J**

Earth people and natives of the planet Ziax unite to find out why water is disappearing from the planet.

•* Sanders, Scott Russell. *Meeting Trees*, illustrated by Robert Hynes. Washington, DC: National Geographic Society, 1997. **PJ+**

While walking in a forest, a father and son share their knowledge about trees.

- Schimmel, Schimm. *Dear Children of the Earth*, illustrated by the author. Minocqua, WI: Northword Press, 1994. **PJ+**

Mother Earth writes a letter asking people to take care of her.

- Smith, Doris Buchanan. *Best Girl.* New York: Viking, 1993. **J+**

Trying to cope with a difficult home life, 11-year-old Nealy takes comfort in her artwork and her care for living things, such as a 100-year-old tree the city wants to cut down.

- Thompson, Julian F. *Gypsyworld.* New York: Henry Holt, 1992. **YA**

A group of teenagers are kidnapped and taken to a parallel world where the environment is not abused, in order to convince people to solve the earth's environmental problems.

•* Van Allsburg, Chris. *Just a Dream*, illustrated by the author. Boston: Houghton Mifflin, 1990. **J+**

Walter's dream helps him understand the importance of taking care of the environment.

- Wrightson, Patricia. *Moon-Dark*, illustrated by Noela Young. New York: Margaret K. McElderry Books/Macmillan, 1987. **J+**

  When people begin to settle land formerly occupied by wildlife, the animal inhabitants call on an ancient moon spirit to help save their territory from the humans who are upsetting the ecological balance.

Nonfiction/Informational

Most of these books include information on conservation and/or provide activities to further explore the topic of ecology. Also listed are books that will help educators teach ecology. In a few of these, grade levels are listed in the title.

- Allen, Dorothea. *Hands on Science!: 112 Easy-to-Use, High-Interest Activities for Grades 4–8.* West Nyack, NY: The Center for Applied Research in Education, 1991. **J+**

- Anderson, Joan. *Earth Keepers*, photographs by George Ancona. San Diego: Harcourt Brace Jovanovich, 1993. **J**

- Bellamy, David. *How Green Are You?*, illustrated by Penny Dann. New York: Clarkson N. Potter, 1991. **PJ**

- Bellamy, David. *Tomorrow's Earth: A Squeaky-Green Guide*, illustrated by Benoit Jacques. Philadelphia: Courage, 1992. **J**

- Caduto, Michael J., and Joseph Bruchac. *Keepers of the Earth: Native American Stories and Environmental Activities for Children*, illustrated by John Kahionhes Fadden and Carol Wood. Golden, CO: Fulcrum, 1989. **J**

- Caduto, Michael J., and Joseph Bruchac. *Keepers of Life: Discovering Plants Through Native American Stories and Earth Activities for Children*, illustrated by John Kahionhes Fadden et al. Golden, CO: Fulcrum, 1994. **J**

- Children of the World in Association with the United Nations. *Rescue Mission Planet Earth: A Children's Edition of Agenda 21.* London: Kingfisher, 1994. **J+**

- Dashefsky, H. Steven. *Kids Can Make a Difference! Environmental Science Activities*, illustrated by Debra Ellinger. New York: McGraw-Hill, 1995. **J**

- Dehr, Roma, and Ronald M. Bazar. *Good Planets Are Hard to Find: An Environmental Information Guide: Dictionary and Action Book for Kids (and Adults)*, illustrated by Nola Johnston. Vancouver, BC: Earth Beat Press, 1990. **J+**

- DeVito, Alfred, and Gerald H. Krockover. *Creative Sciencing: Ideas and Activities for Teachers and Children (Grades K–8)*. Glenview, IL: Scott, Foresman, 1991. **PJ+**

- Drutman, Ava Deutsch, and Susan Klam Zuckerman. *Protecting Our Planet: Activities to Motivate Students to a Better Understanding of Our Environmental Problems (for Grades 4–8)*, illustrated by Christine Kluge. Carthage, IL: Good Apple, 1991. **J+**

- Dudley, William. *The Environment: Distinguishing Between Fact and Opinion.* San Diego: Greenhaven, 1990. **J**

•* The EarthWorks Group (edited by Catherine Dee). *Kid Heroes of the Environment*, illustrated by Michele Montez. Berkeley, CA: EarthWorks Press, 1991. **J+**

  Choose one or two stories as an alternative read-aloud.

- The EarthWorks Group (and John Javna). *50 Simple Things Kids Can Do to Save the Earth*, illustrated by Michele Montez. Kansas City, MO: Andrews & McMeel, 1990. **PJ+**

- Elkington, John, Julia Hailes, Douglas Hill, and Joel Makower. *Going Green: A Kid's Handbook to Saving the Planet*, illustrated by Tony Ross. New York: Puffin, 1990. **J+**

- Galle, Janet R., and Patricia A. Warren. *Ecology Discovery Activities Kit: A Complete Teaching Unit for Grades 4–8*, illustrated by Arek W. Galle. West Nyack, NY: Center for Applied Research Education, 1989. **J+**

- Gardner, Robert. *Celebrating Earth Day: A Sourcebook of Activities and Experiments*, illustrated by Sharon Lane Holm. Brookfield, CT: Millbrook Press, 1992. **J+**

- Gartner, Robert. *Careers Inside the World of Environmental Science*, photographs by AP/Wide World. New York: Rosen Publishing Group, 1995. **YA**

- Goodman, Billy. *A Kid's Guide to How to Save the Planet*, illustrated by Paul Meisel. New York: Avon, 1990. **J**

- Holmes, Anita. *I Can Save the Earth: A Kid's Handbook for Keeping Earth Healthy and Green*, illustrated by David Neuhaus. New York: Julian Messner, 1993. **J**

- * Jeffers, Susan (illustrator). *Brother Eagle, Sister Sky: A Message from Chief Seattle.* New York: Dial, 1991. **PJ+**

- Langone, John. *Our Endangered Earth: What We Can Do to Save It*, illustrated by Leslie Cober. Boston: Little, Brown, 1992. **YA**

- Lowery, Linda. *Earth Day*, illustrated by Mary Bergherr. Minneapolis: Carolrhoda, 1991. **J**

- Lowery, Linda, and Marybeth Lorbiecki. *Earthwise at Home: A Guide to the Care & Feeding of Your Planet*, illustrated by David Mataya, photographs from various sources. Minneapolis: Carolrhoda, 1993. **J**

- Lowery, Linda, and Marybeth Lorbiecki. *Earthwise at Play: A Guide to the Care & Feeding of Your Planet*, illustrated by David Mataya, photographs from various sources. Minneapolis: Carolrhoda, 1993. **J**

- Lowery, Linda, and Marybeth Lorbiecki. *Earthwise at School: A Guide to the Care & Feeding of Your Planet*, illustrated by David Mataya, photographs from various sources. Minneapolis: Carolrhoda, 1993. J

- Markle, Sandra. *The Kids' Earth Handbook*, illustrated by the author, photographs from various sources. New York: Atheneum, 1991. **J**

- Metzger, Mary, and Cinthya P. Whittaker. *This Planet Is Mine: Teaching Environmental Awareness and Appreciation to Children.* New York: Fireside, 1991. **J**

- Miles, Betty. *Save the Earth: An Action Handbook for Kids*, illustrated by Nelle Davis, photographs from various sources. New York: Knopf, 1991. **J+**

- Pearce, Fred. *The Big Green Book*, illustrated by Ian Winton. New York: Grosset & Dunlap, 1991. **J**

- Pedersen, Anne. *The Kids' Environment Book: What's Awry and Why*, illustrated by Sally Blakemore. Santa Fe, NM: John Muir, 1991. **J**

- Porritt, Jonathon. *Captain Eco and the Fate of the Earth*, illustrated by Ellis Nadler. New York: Dorling Kindersley, 1991. **PJ**

- Pringle, Laurence. *Taking Care of the Earth: Kids in Action*, illustrated by Bobbie Moore. Honesdale, PA: Boyds Mills Press, 1996. **J+**

- Schwartz, Linda. *Earth Book for Kids: Activities to Help Heal the Environment*, illustrated by Beverly Armstrong. Santa Barbara, CA: Learning Works, 1990. **J**

- Scott, Michael. *The Young Oxford Book of Ecology*, photographs from various sources. New York: Oxford University Press, 1995. **YA**

- Wilkes, Angela. *My First Green Book*, photographs by Dave King and Mike Dunning. New York: Knopf, 1991. **J**

- Zeff, Robbin Lee. *Environmental Action Groups*, photographs from various sources. New York: Chelsea House, 1994. **J+**

Program Plan

GUEST READER

Basketball player/coach.

HOW TO FIND THE GUEST READER

- Contact the professional basketball team's organization in your area. Ask to speak to the Speakers Bureau or the Community Affairs/Public Relations Department or ask them to direct you to the appropriate department.
- Call the athletic or physical-education department of the local university, college, high school, or recreation center.
- Contact the organizations listed below for referrals (many of these groups may also be able to help young people find a local league to join or provide some guidance regarding official rules):

  All American Red Heads
  (touring women's team)
  P.O. Box 100
  Caraway, AR 72419
  (501) 482-3922

  Amateur Athletic Union
  c/o The Walt Disney World Resort
  P.O. Box 10000

Lake Buena Vista, FL 32830-1000
(407) 363-6170

Continental Basketball Association
701 Market Street, Suite 140
St. Louis, MO 63101-1824
(303) 331-0404

Harlem Globetrotters
6121 Santa Monica Boulevard
Hollywood, CA 90038
(213) 461-5400

Naismith Memorial Basketball Hall of Fame
1150 W. Columbus Avenue
P.O. Box 179
Springfield, MA 01101
(413) 781-6500

National Amateur Basketball Association
6832 W. North Avenue, Suite 4A
Chicago, IL 60635
(312) 637-0811

National Association of Basketball Coaches of the United States
9300 W. 110th Street, Suite 640
Overland Park, KS 66210-1486
(913) 469-1001

National Association Intercollegiate Athletics
6120 S. Yale, Suite 1450
Tulsa, OK 74136
(918) 494-8828

National Basketball Association (NBA)
645 Fifth Avenue, 10th Floor
New York, NY 10022
(212) 826-7000

National Collegiate Athletic Association (NCAA)
6201 College Boulevard
Overland Park, KS 66211
(913) 339-1906

National Federation of State High School Association
11724 Northwest Plaza Circle

P.O. Box 20626
Kansas City, MO 64195-0626
(816) 464-5400

National Wheelchair Basketball Association
University of Kentucky
110 Seaton Building
Lexington, KY 40506-0219
(606) 257-1623

U.S. Olympic Committee
1 Olympic Plaza
Colorado Springs, CO 80909-5760
(719) 632-5551

USA Basketball
5465 Mark Dabling Boulevard
Colorado Springs, CO 80918-3842
(719) 590-4800

Women's Basketball Coaches Association
4646 B Lawrenceville Highway
Lilburn, GA 30247
(404) 279-8027

Canadian Amateur Basketball Association
1600 James Naismith Drive
Gloucester, ON K1B 5N4, Canada
(613) 746-0060

ESTIMATED TIME

45 minutes–1 hour.

READ-ALOUD BOOK

For the Love of the Game: Michael Jordan and Me, by Eloise Greenfield, illustrated by Jan Spivey Gilchrist. New York: HarperCollins, 1997.

Basketball and Michael Jordan's dedication to the game is a metaphor for life's challenges and joys in this beautifully written and illustrated book.

BEFORE THE VISIT

- Decorate the room with posters of famous players "in action."
- Decorate the room with basketballs and basketball t-shirts cut out of construction paper. Print the name of each student in the class on a basketball or shirt.
- Reserve the basketball court in the school's gymnasium or on the playground.
- Reserve any equipment the Guest Reader may need, such as a basketball, screen, or projector for slides or a video-cassette recorder.

INTRODUCTION OF THE GUEST READER

"In basketball, the moves make the man or the woman. To show us the right moves is our Guest Reader (team name) superstar, (Guest Reader's name)!"

GUEST READER'S INTRODUCTION OF THE BOOK

"Basketball coaches look for players who have talent, skill, and the willingness to work hard. In this book, *For the Love of the Game: Michael Jordan and Me* by Eloise Greenfield, two children discover the importance of the human spirit and the importance of working hard to develop their talents—even when the going gets rough!"

DISCUSSION TOPICS

Suggest to the Guest Reader to:

- Present a brief history of basketball. In 1891, James Naismith, a physical education teacher at the YMCA Training School in Springfield, Massachusetts, knew how bored his students were after football season. Because of the winter weather, they usually did calisthenics indoors every day, and they wanted a more inter- esting physical activity. Dr. Naismith invented the game to meet this need. He nailed a peach basket to the balcony at each end of the gym. The players used a soccer ball. When a goal was finally made, a custodian had to climb a ladder to retrieve the ball! The game is named after the peach baskets. The Basketball Hall of Fame is now located in Springfield, where the game was invented.

- Explain that basketball is considered to be a truly all-American sport invented in America for Americans. Baseball evolved from "rounders," a British game; football from soccer and rugby, also British games; tennis was developed by French clerics, etc.

- Explain that basketball is one of the most popular international sports. Baseball and football are played in a few other countries, but basketball is not only an Olympic sport, it is played throughout the world—in over 130 countries. One reason it is so popular is because of its simplicity. All you need is a ball and a hoop. Officially, basketball has five players on court per team, but you can informally play with less people or if no one is around, you can even play basketball by yourself.

- Describe how he became interested in basketball, and how he prepared to pursue this interest.

- Emphasize the importance of preparation, practice, maintaining a healthy life-style, and working toward a goal for success in sports and in life. Stress also the importance of an education and reading.

- Either wear a uniform or show the uniform and equipment. Explain that the uniform must be loose so it does not restrict movement. The shoes have either a high- or low-ankle support and a thick sole. Jumping and running causes pounding on a player's feet and legs. Thick soles help absorb these shocks. Thick socks help prevent blisters.

DEMONSTRATION

- Briefly summarize the purpose and rules of the game and the names of the markings on the court.

- Give a demonstration of basketball skills. The demo might include how to dribble the ball; different ways to pass, such as the chest pass, bounce pass, overhead pass; and how to shoot, such as a lay-up shot, jump shot, and hook shot. If possible, include a few students in the demonstration. (Michael Cooper, former Los Angeles Lakers player and currently a member of the Los Angeles

Lakers organization, was the Guest Reader who visited my school. After going over the finer points of shooting, passing, etc., he invited three or four children to play against him—a little "four on one." The young players and spectators were ecstatic!)

- If a "live" demonstration is not possible, ask the Guest Reader to bring a video that shows basketball action.

Note: Unless it is logistically impossible, ask the Guest Reader to read the story and to talk about basketball in the classroom before moving to the basketball court for the demonstration.

KIDS' ACTIVITIES

Ask the students to:

- Learn the terminology of the game, such as dribble, key, point guard, zone defense, etc. Create word puzzles, such as word jumbles or cross-word puzzles.
- Learn the basic rules of basketball and basketball history. If there is time, also review a few of the official basketball signals that the referees use. (Descriptions of signals can be found in books such as *The Illustrated Rules of Basketball* by Frank Bennett; *Youth Basketball* by Karen Garchow and Amy Dickinson; and *Basketball Rules in Pictures* by A. G. Jacobs.) Organize a quiz game to test the contestants' knowledge of the rules, terms, history, and signals. Give a prize to the team that wins.
- Draw a timeline outlining the history of basketball. Books, such as *The Story of Basketball* by Dave Anderson, provide a great deal of information.
- Improve skills by practicing basketball drills. Here are a few basic drills to begin with:

  –run backwards

  –dribble down court using one hand. Dribble back using the other hand. Then switch hands with each dribble

  –dribble around cones or chairs, weaving between them

  –face a partner standing on opposite foul lanes. Practice a bounce pass, chest pass, and overhead pass with your partner

For additional drills, refer to books such as *Play Like a Pro* by James Allen; *Basketball for Young Champions* by Robert J. Antonacci and Jene Barr; *Make the Team, Basketball: A Slammin', Jammin' Guide to Super Hoops!* by Richard J. Brenner; *Beginning Basketball* by Julie Jensen; and *The Young Basketball Player* by Chris Mullin. Books for coaches, such as *Youth Basketball* by Karen Garchow and Amy Dickinson and *The Basketball Coach's Bible* by Sidney Goldstein, also describe drills. In addition, see the **VIDEOS** section for listings of instructional videos. Remember to always warm up before practice and cool down after practice.

- Play games that reinforce shooting skills:

  –*Around the World*—Can be played with friends or alone. Choose seven spots from which to shoot a basket. Usually the player begins near one side of the basket on the foul lane. The foul line is the midway point. Choose two spots between the first spot and the foul-line spot. On the other foul lane, choose three more spots that mirror the first three. After you make a basket from each spot, repeat in reverse. If you are playing with a friend, you take turns. You shoot until you miss. If you miss, you stay at that spot until your next turn. The first to go "around the world" wins

  –*H-O-R-S-E*—Must be played with two or more players. One player makes a shot, such as a jump shot from the foul line. If s/he makes it, the next player must copy it, standing on the same spot. If the second player misses the shot, s/he gets a letter "H." If the second player makes the shot, s/he does not get a letter. If the first player does not make the shot, the second player gets to shoot the ball whatever way s/he likes. Then the first player must duplicate it. The first player to accumulate all the letters H-O-R-S-E, loses.

  These and other games are described in *Play Like a Pro* by James Allen and *Make the Team, Basketball: A Slammin', Jammin' Guide to Super Hoops!* by Richard J. Brenner. Also, view *Basketball Backyard Games,* a video that turns "skill development into fun and games."

- Help organize a basketball team, perhaps competing against another class. Design and make:

–a team pennant

–team uniforms (decorate T-shirts and shorts)

–basketball trading cards with students as the players

Remember to create a team logo to place on these items.

- Help organize shooting contests. Who can throw the basketball the farthest and make a basket? Who can make the most baskets in a set amount of time, such as one minute? (Read about basketball contests in *Sara Kate, Superkid* by Susan Beth Pfeffer and *Slam Dunk Saturday* by Jean Marzollo.) Give a prize to the contest winner. Consider making the contests fundraisers by asking for donations to register for contests or by asking friends to sponsor contestants, pledging money for each basket made, for example.

- With the teacher and classmates, learn first aid. Discuss what to do if a player gets hurt during practice or in a game. Remember, a player should never play through the pain. The book *Youth Basketball* by Karen Garchow and Amy Dickinson has a section about sports medicine and training.

- Be a scorekeeper. Watch a game, live or on television. Keep track of the score, each team's missed shots, and turnovers (when one team loses the ball before shooting at the basket). Keep track of players' assists (when passes to teammates lead to baskets), each individual player's scores and fouls. *The Basketball Coach's Bible* by Sidney Goldstein provides a detailed explanation of how to keep track of the statistics during a game.

- Graph a favorite team's scores. Variation: Graph several teams' scores on a chart and compare.

- Write a sports article describing a game seen on television or live.

- Interview a player on the class, school, recreation center, or local team. Write a sports-feature article on the player.

- Take a video of a local team game and provide play-by-play narration.

- Create a documentary about the class/school team or a local team. Variation: Film a documentary about one player.

- Write and present a skit that is a parody of a sports news program or sports interview show. The anchor or reporter can describe a current event and/or interview a current player. Variation: They can pretend they are living in the past and are reporting on an important story that actually occurred then. The news segment can include interviews with important basketball personalities from history such as James Naismith. Recruit classmates to play the different roles.

- If they are basketball fans, share with the class the basketball paraphernalia from their own collection, including their own team uniform, team trophies, etc.

- Keep a journal describing their experience as a team player.

- Cut out articles about basketball. Discuss the stories in class. Keep clippings in a scrapbook or in the journal.

- Read biographies of famous players such as Larry Bird, Michael Jordan, Magic Johnson, Sheryl Swoopes, and Lynette Woodard (the first female on the Harlem Globetrotters). There are many books about individual players. There are also a few books with a collection of short biographical sketches such as *Basketball Legends* by Paul J. Deegan, photographs by UPI/Bettmann and Christopher Lauber (Minneapolis: Abdo & Daughters, 1990) and *Rising Stars of the NBA* by Joe Layden, photographs from various sources (New York: Scholastic, 1997). Write a report, story, or poem about one of these athletes.

- Read a book about individual teams such as *Hoops: Behind the Scenes with the Boston Celtics* by Brendan Boyd and Robert Garrett, photographs by Henry Horenstein (Boston: Little Brown, 1989); *Chicago Bulls* by Michael E. Goodman, photographs from various sources (Mankato, MN: Creative Education, 1993); *Los Angeles Clippers* by Richard Rambeck, photographs from various sources (Mankato, MN: Creative Education, 1993). Write a report, story, or poem about one of these teams.

- Write an essay, story, or poem about their favorite team or player. Explain why their choice is their favorite.

- Write a fan letter to a player. Usually a team will forward mail to its players. For addresses of teams and players, check out *How to Reach Your Favorite Sports Star III* by Dylan B. Tomlinson (Los Angeles: Lowell House Juvenile, 1996); *The Kids' Address Book* by Michael Levine (New York: Perigee/Berkley Publishing Group, 1994); *The Address Book* by Michael Levine (New York: Perigee/

Berkley Publishing Group, 1995); or the *Sports Address Bible: The Comprehensive Directory of Sports Addresses* by Edward Kobak (Santa Monica, CA: Global Sports Productions, 1996), which is found in the reference section of many libraries.

- Create a mobile or a book that presents facts, statistics, and pictures of players. Some interesting trivia includes:

  –Who is the only NBA player to score 100 points in one game? *Answer*: Wilt Chamberlain

  –Why is a basketball court sometimes referred to as a cage and basketball as the "caged game"? *Answer*: Because in the early days of professional basketball, the court was enclosed in netting to separate the players from the spectators.

  –Why is the rim of the basket 10 feet above the floor? *Answer*: Because when James Naismith originated the game, he hung the peach baskets from a balcony 10 feet off the floor.

  Find these and other facts in books such as *The Kids' World Almanac of Basketball* by Bill Gutman; *Hoopmania! The Jam-Packed Book of Basketball Trivia* by Brad Herzog; *The NBA Book of Fantastic Facts, Feats & Super Stats* by Zander Hollander; *Beginning Basketball* by Julie Jensen; *Fabulous Forwards* by Marty Nabhan; *Great Guards* by Marty Nabhan; and *Men in the Middle* by Marty Nabhan.

- Read a poem about basketball (see **POETRY**), and write a poem about basketball from the viewpoint of a player, coach, or spectator.

- Write an essay, story, or poem about an important game (not necessarily basketball) they were involved in. Were they nervous? Stressed? Excited?

- As discussed in the book, *For the Love of the Game: Michael Jordan and Me* by Eloise Greenfield, there are sometimes obstacles that must be surmounted to reach a goal. Write an essay, story, or poem about a time this happened in their life (it does not necessarily have to be sports related).

- Write an essay describing their strengths and talents, and what they need to do to develop them. What are they currently doing to reach their goal?

- Read the story about Magic Johnson's embarrassing debut with the Los Angeles Lakers in the books *The Basketball Hall of Shame* and/or *The Basketball Hall of Shame, Kids' Edition* by Bruce Nash and Allan Zullo. Write an essay, story, or poem about their most embarrassing moment (it does not have to be sports related).

- Read *Red-Hot Hightops* by Matt Christopher and *Crane's Rebound* by Alison Jackson. Do they have "lucky" shoes, a "magic" basketball, or any lucky charms and superstitions like the characters in these books? Write about their talisman and why it gives them confidence. Or write an essay about others who have lucky charms. Variation: Write an essay about why they may think a lucky charm or superstitious behavior is silly.

- Read books such as *The Moves Make the Man* by Bruce Brooks; *The Basket Counts* by Matt Christopher; *Smitty* by Bill Gutman; *Nothing But Net, Point Guard, On the Line*—all by Dean Hughes; *Blowing Bubbles With the Enemy* by Alison Jackson; *Backyard Basketball Superstar* by Monica Klein; *All It Takes is Practice* by Betty Miles; *Hoops* by Walter Dean Myers; *The Outside Shot* by Walter Dean Myers; *Taking Sides* by Gary Soto; *Yea! Wildcats!* and *A City for Lincoln,* both by John R. Tunis. These books and others deal with issues of prejudice and discrimination because of gender, race, or social class. Write about any experiences they may have had dealing with prejudice and discrimination. Or have they ever felt prejudice against someone else? (The story does not have to be sports related.)

- Take photos of individual teammates and a group photo of the team. Create a display or collage of these photos, or blow them up to poster size to decorate the classroom.

- Like the famous sports artist LeRoy Neiman, paint a portrait of a player or a picture of players in action.

- Draw a self-portrait in which they are participating in a favorite sport.

- Create a basketball collage using article clippings, headlines, photos from newspapers and magazines, and fabrics that represent a favorite team's colors.

- Design and create awards, trophies, or medals.

- Create a diorama of a basketball court. Label the markings and areas of the court. If possible, add players and spectators.
- Discuss careers in basketball. Check out books on this subject in **RELATED BOOKS**.

VIDEOS

Instructional Videos

- *Basketball Backyard Games,* with John Scott (Basketball Fundamentals/Converse, 1991. 30 minutes)
- *Basketball for All Ages with Paul Westphal* (Schoolmasters Video, 1991. 25 minutes)
- *Basketball of the 90's: Beginning Basketball with Bibby,* with Coach Henry Bibby of the Tulsa Fast Breakers, CBA (Allied Video, 1990. 57 minutes)
- *Becoming a Basketball Player* series with Coach Hal Wissel of Springfield College. This video includes "Ball Handling"; "Shooting"; "Offensive Moves"; "Dribble"; "Defense and Rebounding." (The Athletic Institute, 1990. 20 minutes)
- *Dr. J's Basketball Stuff* with Julius Erving (CBS Fox Company, 1987. Running time not stated)

Documentary Video

- *Harlem Globetrotters: Six Decades of Magic* (Fries Home Video, 1988. 60 minutes)

Films on Video

- *Annie O,* starring Coco Yares, Chad Willett, Rob Stewart (Showtime presents a Sugar Entertainment Production/ Hallmark Home Entertainment, 1995. 93 minutes. Rated PG)

  Fifteen-year-old Annie Rojas becomes the first girl to make the all-male high-school varsity team. She must deal with resentment from teammates, parents, boyfriend, and brother.

- *Hoosiers,* starring Gene Hackman, Barbara Hershey, and Dennis Hopper (Hemdale Film Corp. A Carter De Haven Production

Orion Pictures Release, 1986/Live HomeVideo, Inc. Family Home Entertainment Theatre, 1993. 114 minutes. Rated PG)

Set in 1950's Indiana, a basketball coach leads a low-ranked high-school basketball team to the top.

• *Space Jam,* starring Michael Jordan and Bugs Bunny (Warner Bros. presents an Ivan Reitman/David Falk–Ken Ross Production Warner Bros./Family Entertainment, 1996, 1997. Animated/Live Action Film. 88 minutes Rated PG)

The Tune Squad plays the Nerdlucks in a basketball game to decide if Looney Tunes remain here or become an attraction at a galactic off-ramp called Moron Mountain.

Songs

• "She Likes Basketball," words by Hal David and music by Burt Bacharach, p. 50 in *Promises, Promises* (vocal score of the Broadway musical). n.p.: Edwin H. Morris/New York: Blue Seas Music–Jac Music, 1968.

• "Sweet Georgia Brown," words and music by Ben Bernie, Maceo Pinkard, and Kenneth Casey, p. 239 in *Unforgettable Musical Memories,* edited by William L. Simon. Pleasantville, NY: The Reader's Digest Association, 1984. (There are many recordings by many artists of this song.)

This is the theme song of the novelty basketball team, the Harlem Globetrotters. Founded by Abe Saperstein, the team's first game was in 1927. The Globetrotters have toured all over the world with their special brand of comedic, sleight-of-hand basketball entertainment ever since. Read more about the Harlem Globetrotters in books such as *The Story of Basketball* by Dave Anderson, and view the video *Harlem Globetrotters: Six Decades of Magic.*

Magazines

• *Kidsports*
1101 Wilson Boulevard, Suite 1800
Arlington, VA 22209-2248
(703) 276-3030

- *Sports Illustrated for Kids*
1271 Avenue of the Americas
Rockefeller Center
New York, NY 10020-1393
(212) 522-1212

  For listings of basketball or sports magazines directed to a general audience, see *The Standard Periodical Directory* (New York: Oxbridge Communications) or *Ulrich's International Periodicals Directory* (New Providence, NJ: R.R. Bowker).

POETRY

- "Basketball," by Nikki Giovanni, p. 123 in *The Random House Book of Poetry for Children,* selected by Jack Prelutsky, illustrated by Arnold Lobel. New York: Random House, 1983.

  This can also be found in *Tomie dePaola's Book of Poems,* collected by Tomie dePaola, illustrated by the author (New York: Putnam's, 1988), p. 54.

- "Basketball Star," by Karama Kufuka, p. 123 in *The Random House Book of Poetry for Children.*

- "Basket-Blasting," by Isabel Joshlin Glaser, p. 45 in *Dreams of Glory: Poems Starring Girls,* selected by Isabel Joshlin Glaser, illustrated by Pat Lowery Collins. New York: Atheneum, 1995.

- * "Fernando," by Marci Ridlon, p. 56 in *A New Treasury of Children's Poetry: Old Favorites and New Discoveries,* selected by Joanna Cole, illustrated by Judith Gwyn Brown. Garden City, NY: Doubleday, 1984.

  This can also be found in *The Random House Book of Poetry for Children,* p. 109, and *Slam Dunk: Basketball Poems,* compiled by Lillian Morrison, illustrated by Bill James (New York: Hyperion Books for Children, 1995), p. 22.

- * "Foul Shot," by Edwin Hoey, p. 220 in *The Random House Book of Poetry for Children.*

  This can also be found in *Reflections on a Gift of Watermelon Pickle . . . and Other Modern Verse,* compiled by Stephen Dunning, Edward Lueders, and Hugh Smith, photographs from various sources (New York: Lothrop, Lee & Shepard, 1967), p. 112, and *Slam Dunk: Basketball Poems,* p. 12.

•* "Stringbean Small," p. 60 in *The New Kid on the Block,* by Jack Prelutsky, illustrated by James Stevenson. New York: Greenwillow, 1984.

This can also be found in *Slam Dunk: Basketball Poems,* p. 24.

Poetry Books About Sports

•* *American Sports Poems,* selected by R. R. Knudson and May Swenson. New York: Orchard Books, 1988. Includes poems about basketball:

"Wilt Chamberlain," by R. R. Knudson, p. 22

"Patrick Ewing Takes a Foul Shot," by Diane Ackerman, p. 23 (this is also found in *Slam Dunk: Basketball Poems,* p. 34)

"Anthem," by Stephen Vincent, p. 77

"Song: Take Who Takes You," by Fred Gardner, p. 80

"Lanky Hank Farrow," by Harold Witt, p. 81

"Nothing But Net," by Roy Scheele, p. 82 (this is also found in *Slam Dunk: Basketball Poems,* p. 16)

"Makin' Jump Shots," by Michael S. Harper, p. 83

"Point Guard," by Arnold Adoff, p. 84 (this is also found in *Sports Pages* by Arnold Adoff [see below])

"Fast Break," by Edward Hirsch, p. 85

"Ex-Basketball Player," by John Updike, p. 87

"Basketball : A Retrospective," by Stephen Dunn, p. 88 (this is also found in *Slam Dunk: Basketball Poems,* p. 55)

•* *Sports Pages,* by Arnold Adoff, illustrated by Steve Kuzma. New York: Harper & Row, 1986. Includes poems about basketball:

"Point Guard," p. 32 (this is also found in *American Sports Poems*)

"My Short Story," p. 36

"Afternoons: Four," p. 38

Choose one or two poems from either of these books for an alternative read-aloud.

The following book is an anthology of poetry about basketball. It also includes biographies of players and their statistics:

•* *Slam Dunk: Poems About Basketball.*

Choose one or two poems as an alternative read-aloud.

RELATED BOOKS

Fiction

- Birdseye, Tom. *Tarantula Shoes.* New York: Holiday House, 1995. **J**

  An 11-year-old tries to earn money to buy special basketball shoes so that he will feel accepted in his new neighborhood.

- Brooks, Bruce. *The Moves Make the Man.* New York: HarperCollins, 1984. **YA**

  A young black basketball player and an emotionally troubled white boy form a friendship.

- Cebulash, Mel. *Flipper's Boy,* illustrated by Duane Krych. Mankato, MN: Child's World, 1993. **J+**

  Although he is happy to be a starter on his basketball team, Tommy resents being compared to his father, who deserted the family when Tommy was very young.

- Christopher, Matt. *The Basket Counts,* illustrated by Karen Meyer Swearingen. Boston: Little, Brown, 1991. **J**

  Mel tries to overcome the prejudice of a basketball teammate.

- Christopher, Matt. *Johnny Long Legs,* illustrated by Harvey Kidder. Boston: Little, Brown, 1970. **J**

  Even though he is the tallest member on his basketball team, a young boy discovers he is not the best player.

- Christopher, Matt. *Red-Hot Hightops,* illustrated by Paul D. Mock. Boston: Little, Brown, 1987. **J**

  Kelly becomes a confident basketball player when she wears a mysterious pair of sneakers that she finds.

- Cooper, Ilene. *Choosing Sides.* New York: Puffin/Penguin, 1990. **J**

  A young boy does not want his father to think he is a quitter, but he is not enjoying being on his middle-school basketball team.

- Draper, Sharon M. *Tears of a Tiger.* New York: Atheneum, 1994. **YA**
  The death of a star high-school basketball player in a car accident affects the lives of others in his school.

- Dygard, Thomas J. *The Rebounder.* New York: Puffin/Penguin, 1996. **YA**
  A tragic accident has made a high-school student decide to never play basketball again.

- Dygard, Thomas J. *Tournament Upstart.* New York: Puffin/Penguin, 1989. **J+**
  A basketball team from the Ozark foothills challenges a big-city school for the state championship.

- Gorman, S. S. *Slam Dunk (The High Fives).* New York: Minstrel/Pocket Books, 1990. **J**
  The "High Five" battle bullies on and off the court.

- Gutman, Bill. *Smitty.* Seattle: Turman, 1988. **YA**
  A talented female basketball player must crack the gender barrier and prove herself to the coach and players in a new high school.

- Halecroft, David. *Benched!* New York: Puffin/Penguin, 1992. **J**
  Two friends allow basketball to come before everything, including homework.

- Hallowell, Tommy. *Jester in the Backcourt.* New York: Viking/Penguin, 1990. **J**
  Nick has to learn to control his antics on the basketball court if his team is to win the championship.

- Herman, Hank. *Super Hoops* series tracking the ups and downs of the basketball players on the Branford Bulls. As of this writing there are fifteen titles in the series, including *Crashing the Boards* (*Super Hoops* no. 1) (New York: Bantam, 1996); *Ball Hog* (*Super Hoops* no. 8) (New York: Bantam, 1996); and *Rebound* (*Super Hoops* no. 15) (New York: Bantam, 1998). **J**

- Hughes, Dean. *Angel Park Hoop Stars Series:* 1. *Nothing But Net* (1992); 2. *Point Guard* (1992); 3. *Go to the Hoop!* (1993); 4. *On the Line* (1993). Series illustrated by Dennis Lyall. New York: Bullseye/Knopf. **J**

No. 1—An African-American boy has trouble fitting in with his basketball team in his new, mostly white neighborhood.

No. 2—A young girl tries to convince the basketball coach that she can play as well as the boys.

No. 3—Assigned to play center on his basketball team, a young boy tries to develop self- confidence.

No. 4—A guard must learn to keep his cool under pressure.

- Hughes, Dean. *One-Man Team.* New York: Bullseye/Knopf, 1994. **J+**

  An eighth-grade basketball player whiz must learn to be a team player.

- Hughes, Dean. *The Trophy.* New York: Knopf, 1994. **J**

  Danny tries to improve as a basketball player while dealing with an alcoholic father.

- Jackson, Alison. *Blowing Bubbles With the Enemy.* New York: Dutton Children's Books, 1993. **J**

  A sixth-grade girl causes tension between the boys and girls at her school when she decides to join a boys' basketball team.

- Jackson, Alison. *Crane's Rebound,* illustrated by Diane Dawson Hearn. New York: Dutton Children's Books, 1991. **J**

  Les must deal with various problems at a summer basketball camp.

- Jackson, Alison. *My Brother the Star,* illustrated by Diane Dawson Hearn. New York: Minstrel/Pocket Books, 1990. **J**

  Competing for attention with his younger brother who is on TV commercials, Les tries out for the county basketball team.

- * Klein, Monica. *Backyard Basketball Superstar,* illustrated by Nola Langner. New York: Pantheon, 1981. **PJ**

  Jeremy wants to choose the best player for his basketball team, and is dismayed to find that the best player is his little sister.

- Kline, Suzy. *Orp Goes to the Hoop.* New York: Putnam's, 1991. **J**

  Orp discovers that the skills he developed in baseball can be transferred to his new sport, basketball.

- Marshall, Kirk. *Hoops Series:* 1. *Fast Breaks*; 2. *Longshot Center*; 3. *Backboard Battle*; 4. *Halfcourt Hero*; 5. *Tourney Fever*; and 6. *Pressure Play.* New York: Ballantine, 1989. **YA**

  No. 1—Brian and his mother move to Indianapolis, where he learns new moves to keep up with his inner-city basketball teammates.

  No. 2—With the help of his coach and a street-wise high-school dropout, Brian learns to perfect his "inside moves."

  No. 3—Psyched out by the competition, Brian goes into a slump.

  No. 4—Two key players are suspended from the team until their grades improve.

  No. 5—The team loses two important players with injuries. Brian must pull the squad together before the tournament.

  No. 6—The team has a chance to win the state championship until their star player is hurt.

- Marzollo, Jean. *Slam Dunk Saturday,* illustrated by Blanche Sims. New York: Stepping Stone/Random House, 1994. **J**

  A young boy who wants to do well at his school's basketball fundraiser is intimidated by a nasty schoolmate.

- Miles, Betty. *All It Takes Is Practice.* New York: Bullseye/Knopf, 1976. **J**

  Stuart discovers what friendship means when racial tension surrounds his new friend from an interracial family.

- Myers Walter Dean. *Hoops.* Laurel-Leaf/Bantam Doubleday Dell, 1983. **YA**

  A teenage basketball player from Harlem is befriended by a former professional player who was forced to quit because of a point-shaving scandal.

- Myers, Walter Dean. *The Outside Shot.* New York: Delacorte, 1984. **YA**

  A boy from Harlem, recruited by a college in the midwest to play basketball, copes with new experiences, including working with a disabled child and dealing with corruption in college sports. This is a sequel to *Hoops.*

- Myers, Walter Dean. *Slam!* New York: Scholastic, 1996. **YA**

  A sixteen-year-old boy counts on his basketball talents to get him out of the inner city.

- Peck, Robert Newton. *Soup's Hoop,* illustrated by Charles Robinson. New York: Delacorte, 1990. **J**

  Soup has crazy plans to help his town's basketball team become victorious.

- Pfeffer, Susan Beth. *Sara Kate, Superkid,* illustrated by Suzanne Hankins. New York: Redfeather/Henry Holt, 1994. **J**

  An "ordinary" eight-year-old girl develops superpowers and can throw a basketball farther than anyone else. Will her superpowers last long enough for her to enter the basketball free-throw contest and win $1,000?

- Porte, Barbara Ann. *Harry's Visit,* illustrated by Yossi Abolafia. New York: Greenwillow, 1983. **PJ**

  Harry does not look forward to visiting his parents' friends.

- Quattlebaum, Mary. *Jackson Jones and the Puddle of Thorns,* illustrated by Melody Rosales. New York: Delacorte, 1994. **J**

  Jackson Jones hopes to earn enough money to buy a basketball.

- Ragz, M. M. *Stiff Competition.* New York: Minstrel/Pocket Books, 1991. **J**

  When his basketball team's sponsor goes out of business, Murphy volunteers to find another, with hilarious results.

- Soto, Gary. *Taking Sides.* San Diego: Harcourt Brace Jovanovich, 1991. **J**

  A young basketball player has divided loyalties when he moves from his Hispanic neighborhood to a white suburban area.

- Stine, R. L. *Be Careful What You Wish For . . .* (Goosebumps no. 12). New York: ApplePaperbacks/Scholastic, 1993. **J**

  Samantha Byrd is a klutz and the laughingstock on her basketball team. When she is granted three wishes by a mysterious woman her life changes, but not for the better.

- Tunis, John R. *A City for Lincoln.* San Diego: Odyssey/Harcourt Brace Jovanovich, 1989. **YA**

A basketball coach who is also the head of the Police Department's Juvenile Aid Division comes up against town politics that threatens his work with the youth and motivates him to run for mayor. This is a sequel to *Yea! Wildcats!*

• Tunis, John R. *Yea! Wildcats!* San Diego: Odyssey/Harcourt Brace Jovanovich, 1989. **YA**

An idealistic basketball coach, taking over a high-school team during mid-season, finds himself at odds with local business and political leaders.

Nonfiction/Informational

Most of these books include information regarding basketball history, terminology, rules, statistics, career guidance, and suggestions for improving skills.

• Aaseng, Nate. *Basketball: You are the Coach,* photographs from various sources. Minneapolis: Lerner, 1983. **J+**

• Aaseng, Nate. *College Basketball: You are the Coach,* photographs from various sources. Minneapolis: Lerner, 1984. **J+**

•* Allen, James. *Basketball: Play Like a Pro.* Mahwah, NJ: Troll, 1990. **J+**

Read the first chapter about the history of basketball as an alternative read-aloud.

•* Anderson, Dave. *The Story of Basketball,* photographs from various sources. New York: Morrow, 1988. **J**

Read the first chapter about the history of basketball as an alternative read-aloud. Must be edited for brevity.

•* Antonacci, Robert J., and Jene Barr. *Basketball for Young Champions,* illustrated by Patti Boyd. New York: McGraw-Hill, 1979. **J**

Read the history of basketball found on pages 4–9 as an alternative read-aloud.

•* Barden, Renardo. *All-Time Greats,* photographs from various sources. Vero Beach, FL: Rourke, 1992. **J+**

Read the first chapter about the history of basketball as an alternative read-aloud.

- Barden, Renardo. *Playoff Pressure,* photographs from various sources. Vero Beach, FL: Rourke, 1992. **J+**

- Bennet, Frank. *The Illustrated Rules of Basketball,* illustrated by Paul Zuehlke. Nashville, TN: Ideals Children's Books, 1994. **PJ+**

- Brenner, Richard J. *Make the Team, Basketball: A Slammin', Jammin' Guide to Super Hoops!,* photographs from various sources. Boston: Little, Brown/A Sports Illustrated for Kids Book, 1990. **J+**

  Read pages 10–11 about the history of basketball as an alternative read-aloud.

- Brooks, Bruce. *NBA by the Numbers,* photographs from the National Basketball Association and various sources. New York: Scholastic, 1997. **PJ**

- Dickmeyer, Lowell A. *Basketball is for Me,* photographs by Alan Oddie. Minneapolis: Lerner, 1980. **J**

- Gutman, Bill. *The Kids' World Almanac of Basketball,* illustrated by Bernard Adnet. Mahwah, NJ: World Almanac Books, 1995. **J+**

- Henderson, Kathy. *I Can Be a Basketball Player,* illustrated by Tom Dunnington, photographs from various sources. Chicago: Childrens Press, 1991. **PJ**

- Herzog, Brad. *Hoopmania! The Jam-Packed Book of Basketball Trivia,* photographs from various sources. New York: A Sports Illustrated for Kids Book/Bantam, 1995. **J+**

- Hollander, Zander. *The NBA Book of Fantastic Facts, Feats & Super Stats,* photographs from various sources. Mahwah, NJ: Troll/Rainbow Bridge, 1996. **J+**

- Jacobs, A. G., editor. *Basketball Rules in Pictures,* illustrated by George Kraynak. New York: Perigee/Putnam's, 1989. **J+**

- * Jensen, Julie. *Beginning Basketball* (adapted from *Fundamental Basketball* by Jim Klinzing and Mike Klinzing), photographs by David Liam Kyle, Andy King, and from various other sources. Minneapolis: Lerner, 1996. **J+**

  Read pages 8–9 about the history of basketball as an alternative read-aloud.

- Layden, Joe. *Dribble, Shoot, Score!,* photographs from various sources. New York: Scholastic, 1997. **J**

- Lerner, Mark. *Careers in Basketball,* photographs by James Schnepf. Minneapolis: Lerner, 1983. **J**

- * Mullin, Chris, with Brian Coleman. *The Young Basketball Player,* photographs by Susanna Price. New York: Dorling Kindersley, 1995. **J**

  Read page 9 on the history of basketball as an alternative read-aloud.

- Nabhan, Marty. *Fabulous Forwards,* photographs from various sources. Vero Beach, FL: Rourke, 1992. **J+**

- Nabhan, Marty. *Great Guards,* photographs from various sources. Vero Beach, FL: Rourke, 1992. **J+**

- Nabhan, Marty. *Men in the Middle,* photographs from various sources. Vero Beach, FL: Rourke, 1992. **J+**

- Preller, James. *NBA Action from A to Z,* photographs from various sources. New York: Scholastic, 1997. **PJ**

- Sullivan, George. *Center,* illustrated by Don Madden, photographs by George Sullivan and Aime LaMontagne. New York: Crowell, 1988. **J**

Books That Include Unusual But True Stories About Basketball

Choose a story from one of these books as an alternative read-aloud.

- * Cebulash, Mel. *Basketball Players Do Amazing Things,* photographs from various sources. New York: Step-Up Books/Random House, 1976. **J**

- * Hollander, Phyllis, and Zander Hollander. *Amazing But True Sports Stories,* photographs from various sources. New York: Scholastic, 1986. YA

- * Liss, Howard. *The Giant Book of Strange But True Sports Stories,* illustrated by Joe Mathieu. New York: Random House, 1976. **J+**

•* Liss, Howard. *The Giant Book of More Strange But True Sports Stories*, illustrated by Joe Mathieu. New York: Random House, 1983. **J+**

•* Nash, Bruce, and Allan Zullo. *The Basketball Hall of Shame*, photographs from various sources. New York: Pocket Books, 1991. **YA**

•* Nash, Bruce, and Allan Zullo. *The Basketball Hall of Shame: Young Fans' Edition*, photographs from various sources. New York: Archway Paperback/Pocket Books, 1993. **YA**

•* Nash, Bruce, and Allan Zullo. *The Greatest Sports Stories Never Told*, illustrated by John Gampert. New York: Simon & Schuster Books for Young Readers, 1993. **J**

Books That Provide Guidelines for Coaches

These books are primarily geared to adults.

• Garchow, Karen, and Amy Dickinson. *Youth Basketball: A Complete Handbook*. Dubuque, IA: Brown/Benchmark, 1992.

• Goldstein, Sidney. *The Basketball Coach's Bible*. Philadelphia: Golden Aura, 1994.

Program  Plan

GUEST READER

Banker.

HOW TO FIND THE GUEST READER

- Contact your local bank.
- Contact the American Bankers Association for a referral. This organization sponsors the ABA Educational Foundation, which educates schoolchildren about banking:

  American Bankers Association
  1120 Connecticut Avenue
  Washington, DC 20036
  (202) 663-5000

ESTIMATED TIME

30 minutes–1 hour.

READ-ALOUD BOOK

Alexander, Who Used to Be Rich Last Sunday, by Judith Viorst, illustrated by Ray Cruz. New York: Aladdin Books/Macmillan Publishing, 1978.

Who wouldn't be able to identify with Alexander—a boy who is easily parted with his money? We all know how it is to absolutely, positively need to buy certain items, even if it is a one-eyed bear, not-a-
full deck of cards, and a melted candle. And we can all sympathize
with having money fall through a crack or having to pay a fine for
small infractions. This humorous book will bring a chuckle to kids
of all ages.

However, if you think this read-aloud is too juvenile for your
group, consider the following alternative:

"Genuine as a Three-Dollar Bill," pages 104–106 in *Destiny,* by Paul
Aurandt. New York: Morrow, 1983.

A real-life account originally heard on the radio series *Paul Harvey—The Rest of the Story,* this tale describes United States currency
before it was standardized in the now-familiar forms. The surprise
ending is a lot of fun and will "accrue" interest in the history of
money.

Before the Visit

Decorate the room with cut-outs of banknotes and coins from all
over the world. Remember to label each. Hang cut-outs of dollar
and cent signs from the ceiling.

Introduction of the Guest Reader

"If you want to buy a bike, purchase new clothes, or go on a long
trip and there's no money in your pocket, and there's no money
hidden in your mattress—where ya gonna go? Straight to the bank!
(Guest Reader's name) from (name of bank) will tell us about the
banking system, and I know he will make a lot of 'cents'!"

Guest Reader's Introduction of the Book

For "Alexander, Who Used to Be Rich Last Sunday"

"How many of you have an allowance? Raise your hands. Many of
you save your money by putting it in a piggy bank or in a savings
account at your local bank. But some of you probably spend the
money right away! It's not always easy to hold onto your money.

That's what Alexander finds out in this book, *Alexander, Who Used to Be Rich Last Sunday* by Judith Viorst."

For "Genuine as a Three-Dollar Bill" from "Destiny"

"We've all heard the expression—it's as phony as a three-dollar bill. That's because only six bills are in common, everyday use in the United States—the one dollar, five dollar, ten dollar, twenty dollar, fifty dollar, and one-hundred dollar bills. There is no three-dollar bill in circulation. But in the past American money was very different, as you will see in this story, "Genuine as a Three-Dollar Bill," from the book *Destiny* by Paul Aurandt.

DISCUSSION TOPICS

Suggest to the Guest Reader to:

- Present a brief history of money and banking:

  A long time ago, people did not need money. They hunted for their food, and they lived in caves or shelters made by themselves. When people began to have specialized skills and began to trade with others, buying and selling took the form of bartering. For example, I will give you one cow for your five loaves of bread. People realized that this could be awkward and cumbersome. During the seventh-century B.C., coins were invented in the kingdom of Lydia, located in present-day Turkey. Paper money was invented in China, probably in the seventh-century A.D. Modern banking began in the 1500's in Italy, although some experts say it began even earlier. Italian bankers conducted their business from benches. The word "bank" comes from the Italian word for bench—*banca*.

- Explain that money is anything that the people agree to place a value on and use in trade. A long time ago, some groups used feathers, beads, or stones as money. Nowadays, money usually comes in two forms, coins and paper. Paper money comes in handy because a lot of coins can be very heavy.

- Describe additional forms of exchange, such as checks, money orders, travelers checks, credit cards, etc. In addition, discuss electronic banking and automated teller machines.

- Discuss the virtues of saving money and spending wisely.
- Explain why it is better to put money in the bank rather than saving large sums in a piggy bank. Include the following points:

  –the bank is safer. It has a security system. Additionally, if the money is stolen or if the bank goes out of business, depositors are still guaranteed to get their money back by the Federal Deposit Insurance Corporation (FDIC) for up to $100,000.

  –money grows in a savings account because of the interest earned.

- Describe the two main types of accounts:

  –savings accounts, where you earn interest (explain interest)

  –checking accounts

- Briefly describe additional banking services such as loans, investment programs, special savings plans, safe deposit boxes, etc.

DEMONSTRATION

Show what a deposit slip, a withdrawal slip, a passbook, a bank statement, and checks look like. Explain how to fill out a check. Use two students in the class when writing in the names on the check.

KIDS' ACTIVITIES

Ask the students to:

- Learn terminology such as dividend, interest, certificates of deposit (CD's), mortgage, inflation, recession, depression, Federal Reserve System, numismatics. Create word puzzles and games.
- List sayings and figures of speech relating to money. Discuss what they think these sayings mean. Do they agree or disagree with some of these philosophies? Examples:

  –nest egg

  –money doesn't grow on trees

  –I'm not made of money

  –money can't buy happiness

  –money makes the world go 'round

–the best things in life are free

–a penny saved is a penny earned

–save for a rainy day

–live for today, tomorrow will take care of itself

–the buck stops here.

Try to think of other sayings.

- List nicknames for money such as dough, bread, smackers, greenbacks, bucks, moola, pictures. Think of other nicknames or create new ones.

- Create a poster or an illustrated booklet describing the derivations of money words such as:

  –*money and mint:* in ancient Rome, coins were made in the temple dedicated to the goddess Juno. Juno's surname was *Moneta,* from which comes the words money and the place for making it, mint.

  –*pecuniary:* animals were often used as a medium of exchange. Pecuniary, which means "relating to money," comes from the Latin word *pecus*—a herd of animals.

  –*salary:* in ancient Rome, soldiers often received salt as their payment. The Latin word for salt is *salarium.*

  –*dollar:* in the 1500's, a large silver coin called the *tyrolian* was minted in Joachimsthal, Bohemia. It soon became known as a *Joachimsthaler,* shortened to *thaler.* In English, it became known as "dollar." Later, during the height of the Spanish Empire, a coin worth eight reales was used throughout the world. It was called the Spanish dollar. The word "dollar" was then adopted in many different countries, including our own.

  –*pieces of eight and bits:* the Spanish silver coins were sometimes called "pieces of eight." To make change, these coins were cut into smaller pieces and became known as "bits."

  –*buck:* in the early days of America, buckskins were often used as the medium of exchange.

  –*greenbacks:* in 1862 the United States government issued its first paper money, which was printed on green paper—thus "greenbacks." However, even though greenbacks were in circulation, many banks still printed their own banknotes. (See "Genuine as a Three-Dollar Bill.")

–*piggy bank:* according to *The Kid's Guide to Money: Earning It, Saving It, Spending It, Growing It, Sharing It* by Steve Otfinoski, in fifteenth century England there were two meanings for the word "pig" or pygg, as it was spelled then: one meant the animal, and the other described a piece of crockery, a container made of clay. Eventually the two meanings were combined. *Money* by Joe Cribb points to seventeenth-century German piggy banks as the earliest examples in Europe, although earlier examples have been reported dating from fourteenth-century Indonesia. Information about the piggy bank can also be found in *Mistakes That Worked* by Charlotte Foltz Jones, illustrated by John O'Brien (New York: Doubleday, 1991), pp. 36–38.

The derivation of money words was culled from the books listed in **RELATED BOOKS**.

- Show their piggy banks to their classmates. (For security reasons, be sure they leave their money at home.)
- Make piggy banks. Decorate a box with wrapping paper, stickers, or markers. Carefully cut a slot into the lid (or use a tissue box). Variation: Paint the box pink. Create a pig face on one end (use pink felt for the ears). Use a small paper cup as the pig nose. Paint it pink and attach it to the pig face. Use a pink pipe cleaner as the tail. Attach it to the opposite end of the box. (To carry out the theme, ask young children to read *Piggy Bank Gonzales* by Jack Kent.)
- Create a "money tree." Attach sticks or twigs onto construction paper or poster board so that it looks like a tree. Attach play money to the "branches" so that they look like leaves. Variation: Decorate a flower pot or a carton. Place sand in the bottom of the pot. Place a stick in the sand so that it stands upright. Attach branches to the stick and play-money to the branches. (To carry out the theme, read *The Money Tree* by Sarah Stewart.)
- Create a poster, a collage, or an illustrated booklet depicting "unusual money" used throughout the history of the world, such as wampum (shells made into belts of beads used by North American Indians and American colonists), fishhooks, animal skins, feathers, tobacco, salt, manillas (lead and copper rings used in European trade with Africa), playing cards (used in Canada), stone disks (used by the people of Yap, an island in the Pacific

ocean. The largest disks measured up to 12 feet across). For additional examples read books such as *All Kinds of Money* by David A. Adler; *Marvels of the U.S. Mint* by Oren Arnold; *Money* by Joe Cribb; *Money* by Benjamin Elkin; *Coins & Currency* by Brenda Ralph Lewis; and *The Story of Money* by Betsy Maestro.

- Design their own banknotes and coins.
- Write a report or create a poster describing the steps for making coins and banknotes. For information, read *Marvels of the U.S. Mint*; *Money* by Joe Cribb; and *Coins & Currency*.
- Create a poster or an illustrated booklet describing money from around the world, such as the pound (United Kingdom), franc (France), and peso (Mexico). Discuss Europe's common currency unit, the euro.
- Start a coin or banknote collection. Organize a club at school. To help get started, read *Money and Banking* by Lois Cantwell; *Money* by Joe Cribb; and *Coins & Currency*. For additional information, write to the following organizations:

  The American Numismatic Association
  818 N. Cascade Avenue
  Colorado Springs, CO 80903-3279
  (719) 632-2646

  The American Numismatic Society
  617 W. 155th Street
  New York, NY 10032
  (212) 234-3130

  Numismatics International
  P.O. Box 670013
  Dallas, TX 75367-0013
  (214) 361-7543

  Society of Paper Money Collectors
  P.O. Box 1085
  Florissant, MO 63031
  http://www.spmc.org/contact

- Using paper and crayons, do coin rubbings. Read *The Buck Book: All Sorts of Things to do with a Dollar Bill—Besides Spend It* by Anne Akers Johnson for ideas on how to use bills for paper-folding designs.

- With classmates, identify American coins and bills. Discuss the meaning of the symbols, numbers, wording, and art printed on the money. For information, read books such as *The Go-Around Dollar* by Barbara Johnston Adams; *Marvels of the U.S. Mint* by Oren Arnold; *Money and Banking* by Lois Cantwell; *Money* by Benjamin Elkin; *Money, Money, Money: The Meaning of the Art and Symbols on United States Paper Currency* by Nancy Winslow Parker; and *Straight Talk About Money* by Marion B. Rendon and Rachel Kranz.

- Write a brief history of the people whose portraits appear on American money. Include coins and banknotes that are not in common use or have been discontinued, such as the Susan B. Anthony dollar (coin); the William McKinley $500 bill; the Grover Cleveland $1,000 bill; the James Madison $5,000 bill; the Salmon P. Chase $10,000 bill; and the Woodrow Wilson $100,000 bill. (Only four people who have appeared on money were not Presidents: Alexander Hamilton, Benjamin Franklin, Salmon P. Chase, and Susan B. Anthony.) The Nancy Winslow Parker book provides brief sketches about the people depicted on banknotes.

- Create a timeline, a poster, or an illustrated book outlining the history of money and banking. Variation: Only cover the history of money and banking in the United States. Books listed in **RELATED BOOKS**, such as *Money* by Joe Cribb, *Coins & Currency* by Brenda Ralph Lewis, *The Story of Money* by Betsy Maestro, and *Straight Talk About Money* by Marion B. Rendon and Rachel Kranz, provide information on this topic. When discussing the Gold Rush, learn the song "Oh, Susannah," p. 180 in *From Sea to Shining Sea: A Treasury of American Folklore and Folk Songs* (compiled by Amy L. Cohn, illustrated by various renown artists. New York: Scholastic, 1993).

- Talk about the Great Depression and what steps have been taken to prevent another economic disaster from happening again. Read *Brother, Can You Spare a Dime? The Great Depression, 1929–1933* by Milton Meltzer (New York: Facts On File, 1991. Originally published in a different form by Alfred A. Knopf, 1969). Also, learn the song "Brother, Can You Spare a Dime?" (see **SONGS**). Learn about hobo life during the depression in the essay "Tramp Talk" by Amy L. Cohn, p. 353, and the unofficial anthem of hoboes, the song "Big Rock Candy Mountain" (traditional), p. 354, both in *From Sea to Shining Sea: A Treasury of American Folklore and Folk Songs.*

- Create a poster or illustrated booklet filled with amazing facts about money. For example:

  –all U.S. currency is printed at the Bureau of Printing and Engraving in Washington, DC, and in Fort Worth, Texas. These facilities print 2.5 million bills a day

  –a stack of worn one-dollar bills destroyed in a single year would tower 200 miles into the sky

  –one dollar bills wear out in about 18 months because of so much use

  –if dollars are inadvertently mutilated—chewed by animals, soaked, torn or burned—the Treasury Department will replace the bills if more than half the original remains. If less than half, a government official will inspect the bill to determine if it can be replaced

  –the Secret Service was originally created in 1865 to combat widespread counterfeiting

  –Peter, an eagle that would roost at the United States Mint in Philadelphia, served as the model for the eagle on the silver dollar that was circulated from 1836 to 1839. When he died, Peter was stuffed and mounted and is now on display in the lobby of the Philadelphia Mint

  This information was culled from the books listed in **RELATED BOOKS**.

- Have a barter day in class. Swap personal items or a service with classmates. Read about a similar activity in *Count Your Money with the Polk Street School* by Patricia Reilly Giff. Learn about the barter system in books found in **RELATED BOOKS**.

- Take a survey of how much money kids receive for their allowance. Also, ask what they spend their money on. Report survey results to the class. Create a graph to accompany the report.

- Keep a spending diary and write down expenses for every purchase, no matter how small, then analyze to determine if money is wisely spent. They should also ask themselves if they are impulse buyers, or if they buy things after they are angry or sad. The problems that emerge if a person does not stick to a budget is discussed in the book, *Not for a Billion Gazillion Dollars* by Paula Danziger.

- Create a personal budget. They should determine their weekly income, including earnings and allowance and what they need to spend money on, such as school lunch or bus fare. Deduct expenses from income, and what is left can be saved or spent. For guidance on writing a budget, read books such as *It's My Money: A Kids Guide to the Green Stuff* by Ann Banks; *The Totally Awesome Money Book for Kids and Their Parents* by Adriane G. Berg and Arthur Berg Bochner; *Every Kid's Guide to Making and Managing Money* by Joy Berry; *The Kid's Guide to Money: Earning It, Saving It, Spending It, Growing It, Sharing It* by Steve Otfinoski; *Straight Talk About Money* by Marion B. Rendon and Rachel Kranz; and *A Kid's Guide to Managing Money* by Joy Wilt.

- Create a budget from an adult's perspective. Do research to find out what the average income is in your area. Deduct expenses from the income, such as rent or mortgage payments, utilities, medical bills, transportation, credit-card bills, taxes, etc.

- Become a smart consumer. Choose several items such as groceries and compare costs in different stores. Determine where to get the best buy. Report findings to the class. Read *The Totally Awesome Money Book for Kids and Their Parents* by Adriane G. Berg and Arthur Berg Bochner, *The Kids' Complete Guide to Money* by Kathy S. Kyte, *The Kid's Guide to Money: Earning It, Saving It, Spending It, Growing It, Sharing It* by Steve Otfinoski for information about consumer awareness.

- List ways a smart consumer can save money such as by doing comparison shopping and using coupons and rebates. Discuss this in class. Also, discuss how to research a product before making a big purchase, such as buying a computer. For example, read the magazine *Consumer Reports,* ask an expert for advice, talk to sales people.

- There is the saying, "the best things in life are free." Write an article describing entertainment that is available in the community that costs very little or is free. For a list of free and almost-free offers for kids (stickers, crafts, toys, sports items, etc.) refer to the book *The Official Freebies for Kids* by the editors of *Freebies Magazine,* illustrated by Jessica Schiffman (Los Angeles: Lowell House Juvenile, 1997), and *Freebies Magazine* (see **MAGAZINES**), and the book, *Free Stuff for Kids—1998* (21st ed.) (Minnetonka, MN: Meadowbrook, 1998 [continually updated]).

- Discuss ways that ads and commercials try to "hook" consumers. Some techniques include celebrity endorsements and emotional appeal. Read about this in books such as the ones by Steve Otfinoski, and Marion B. Rendon and Rachel Kranz. Find examples of each technique in magazine ads and radio and television commercials and discuss these with the class. Create advertisements and commercials using these techniques and present them to the class.

- Write a story, essay, or poem about a "shopping blunder" they made. Variation: Interview friends or family about their "shopping blunder." Did they buy something that was not in style, that broke, or was less expensive in another store?

- Watch television shows and films. Think about the messages these programs give about money. For example, sitcom families rarely worry about money, whereas in reality most families do worry. Write down their findings and report to the class. For further discussion on this topic, read *Straight Talk About Money* by Marion B. Rendon and Rachel Kranz.

- Talk about the changing attitudes about money throughout the twentieth century in America. For example, in the 1920s, consumerism and buying on credit were encouraged. In contrast, in the 1960s such materialism was viewed negatively. What is the attitude at the present time? Read *Straight Talk About Money* by Marion B. Rendon and Rachel Kranz for a good discussion about this topic.

- Cut out articles about the Federal Reserve, banks, and the economy. Discuss any current events dealing with the world of finance.

- In class, learn about the banking system. Discuss the different types of checking accounts and savings accounts. Learn how to complete withdrawal and deposit slips, how to write a check, and how to balance a check book. Pretend there is a $100 in a savings account and figure out the interest.

- Practice simple banking transactions. (*Note:* The teacher can give each student "pretend" money at the end of the day for good behavior and grades. Set up a "banking corner" where students can deposit or withdraw this money to buy small items such as erasers, toys, or candy from the teacher. A banking practice kit that includes checks, savings deposit, and withdrawal slips, credit applications, etc., and classroom money can be obtained from many educational supply stores.)

- Discuss how to get a loan from a bank, credit union, and other financial institutions. Create skits depicting what happens when the applicant has a good line of credit or a poor credit history.

- Learn about different types of jobs in the world of finance such as bank manager, teller, loan officer, accountant, broker, etc. Interview someone in the field. Ask the person to describe his/her job, educational background, salary range, etc. Read about careers in finance. The following books will be helpful: *Careers in a Bank* by Mary Davis; *Careers in Banking and Finance* by Patricia Haddock; and *The Banking Book* by Elaine Scott.

- Create a commercial for their own bank, describing its services. This skit can be presented live, on video, or a "radio ad" can be recorded on audio tape. Have classmates play various roles.

- As a class, choose a company to "invest" in. Follow the stock market for a designated period of time and then "sell." Create a graph of the ups and downs of the chosen stock.

- List ways that kids can make money for themselves or for the class. (Try to match interests with possible jobs: A student who likes small children might enjoy babysitting, or a student who is a good swimmer might think about becoming a lifeguard.) Many of the books listed in **RELATED BOOKS**, including *The Kids' Complete Guide to Money* by Kathy S. Kyte, *Making Cents: Every Kid's Guide to Money* by Elizabeth Wilkinson, and *A Kid's Guide to Managing Money* by Joy Wilt provide good ideas. Most of the fiction listed also describes money-making schemes.

- Think of ways to raise funds for charity or for a good cause. Learn how the young characters in *Project Wheels* by Jacqueline Turner

Banks, *Tanya's Big Dream* by Linda Glaser, and *Lily and Miss Liberty* by Carla Stevens earn money to help others.

- Start a business. Write a report describing the type of business; how much "seed money" was needed to get started; how they got the money and who, if any, are the partners. Describe the problems, failures, and successes. Variation: Write about a business they had in the past or about any experiences they had with employment. Read about the success stories of real-life entrepreneurs in *The Fortunate Fortunes* by Nathan Aaseng, photographs by various sources (Minneapolis: Lerner, 1989). This book also provides a good summary of business and banking terms.

- Choose an established business/company and write about its genesis and how it is faring now. Present the report to the class.

- Think about a business, project, or an idea that they had that everyone "poo-pooed," yet turned out to be a success. Write about this experience (it does not have to be related to business). To learn about companies that succeeded despite initial rejection, read *The Rejects: People and Products that Outsmarted the Experts* by Nathan Aaseng, photographs by various sources (Minneapolis: Lerner, 1989).

- The book *The Hundred Penny Box* by Sharon Bell Mathis and the poem "The Coin" by Sara Teasdale describe how a keepsake and memories can be a treasure in a person's life. Write a story, essay, or poem that describes an item that has sentimental value and conjures up loving memories.

- Think about the times they discovered money unexpectedly ("found money"), whether the money was found on the sidewalk, under a sofa cushion, or in a pocket. Draw a picture, write a story, or tell a story to the class about this experience. Read about a similar situation in *Pigs Will Be Pigs* by Amy Axelrod.

- Imagine that they suddenly became millionaires. How would they spend the money?

- Write a story, essay, or poem about how their life might change if they became very rich. Variation: Write about someone they know who did become wealthy. Read about how wealth impacted the lives of characters in the following books and stories: *The Me Inside of Me* by T. Ernesto Bethancourt; *All the Money in the*

World by Bill Brittain; *Rich Mitch* and *Get Rich Mitch!*—both by Marjorie Weinman Sharmat; *How to Get Fabulously Rich* by Thomas Rockwell; and stories based on the Midas legend.

- The characters in *Not for a Billion Gazillion Dollars* by Paula Danziger, *Cally's Enterprise* by Claudia Mills, *Poor Girl, Rich Girl* by Johnniece Marshall Wilson try to earn money for certain things they desire (a computer, a trip, contact lenses). Write a story, essay, or poem about something they would like to purchase and must save their money to buy. Describe the steps they will take to reach their goal.

- In *Cally's Enterprise* by Claudia Mills, Cally realizes she always tries to meet her parents' and other people's expectations instead of following her own interests. Ask themselves if they ever felt this way, and to write a story, essay, or poem about their feelings and how they handled it.

- Is all fair in love, war, and business? Discuss their feelings about business ethics with classmates. Cut out any articles on the topic and share with the class. Read the book, *The Bathwater Gang Gets Down to Business* by Jerry Spinelli, which discusses this subject.

- The characters in books such as *Max Malone Makes a Million* by Charlotte Herman and *Cally's Enterprise* by Claudia Mills learn the secrets of building a successful business, including the importance of advertising and "going where the customers are." Discuss additional ideas with the class.

- The characters in *The Mariah Delany Lending Library Disaster* by Sheila Greenwald, *Henry Reed, Inc.* and *Henry Reed's Baby-Sitting Service*, both by Keith Robertson, must deal with business problems. Write a story, essay, or poem about a business disaster they or someone else they know have experienced.

- In the books *The Gold Coin* by Alma Flor Ada, *Riches* by Esther Hautzig, *Max Malone Makes a Million* by Charlotte Herman, *The Richest Kids in Town* by Peg Kehrer, and *Make Four Million Dollars by Next Thursday* by Stephen Manes, the characters discover that there is more to life than money, including friendship, family, helping other people, and enjoying nature. Write a story, essay, or poem about their feelings on this topic.

Videos

Instructional Videos

- *The Dime* (Little Red Filmhouse, 1970. 15 minutes)
- *Saving With Tom and Martha* (Smartz Factory, 1994. 24 minutes)

Films on Video

- *Blank Check,* starring Brian Bonsall, Karen Duffy, and Miguel Ferrer (Walt Disney Pictures/Walt Disney Home Video, 1994. 93 minutes. Rated PG)

  A crook gives a young boy a blank check as settlement when he runs over the youngster's bike. The boy fills the check in for a million dollars and then goes on a spending spree. Unfortunately, the FBI and the mob are after the loot.

- *The Happiest Millionaire,* starring Fred MacMurray, Tommy Steele, Greer Garson, and Geraldine Page (Walt Disney Pictures/ Walt Disney Home Video, 1967. 145 minutes. Not rated)

  This Disney musical is about an eccentric millionaire (MacMurray) who presides over a Philadelphia mansion where light-hearted chaos reigns.

- *A Million to Juan,* starring Paul Rodriguez, Polly Draper, and Edward James Olmos (The Samuel Goldwyn Company Crystal Sky Communications Prism Pictures/Turner Home Entertainment, 1994. 97 minutes. Rated PG)

  Juan's life changes when a mysterious benefactor hands him a million dollars. He learns that there is more to life than money. This film is based on a Mark Twain story (see **Stories**).

- *Richie Rich,* starring Macaulay Culkin and John Larroquette (Warner Brothers Davis Entertainment/Warner Home Video, 1994. 95 minutes. Rated PG)

  Richie Rich, the richest kid in the world, is likable but isolated. He has everything money can buy except friends until he hits it off with a group of sandlot kids. The film is based on the comic book series.

- *The Toy,* starring Richard Pryor, Jackie Gleason, Scott Schwartz, and Ned Beatty (Columbia Pictures A Ray Stark Production A Richard Donner Film/Good Times Home Video, 1989. 99 minutes. Rated PG)

  An unsuccessful writer agrees to become the hired playmate of a wealthy brat. The child eventually realizes that good friends cannot be bought.

Songs

- "Brother, Can You Spare a Dime?," words by E. Y. Harburg and music by Joe Gorney, p. 180 in *Rise up Singing: The Group Singing Songbook,* edited by Peter Blood and Annie Patterson, illustrated by Kore Loy McWhirter. Bethlehem, PA: A Sing Out Publication, 1992.

- "Can't Buy Me Love," words and music by John Lennon and Paul McCartney (from the film *A Hard Day's Night*), p. 132 in *The Beatles: The First Four Albums From the Original British Collection* Milwaukee, WI: Hal Leonard, n.d.

  This can also be found in *The Complete Beatles Volume I* (Milwaukee, WI: Hal Leonard, 1988), p. 110.

- "I Found a Million Dollar Baby (in a Five-and-Ten-Cent Store)," words by Billy Rose and Mort Dixon and music by Harry Warren (from the film *Funny Lady*), p. 122 in *Hollywood Musicals Year by Year: 1965–1977.* Milwaukee, WI: Hal Leonard, 1995.

- "If I Were a Rich Man," words by Sheldon Harnick and music by Jerry Bock, p. 38 in *Fiddler on the Roof* (vocal score of the Broadway musical). n.p.: Times Square Music/Milwaukee, WI: Hal Leonard, 1965.

- "I've Got Sixpence" (traditional), p. 87 in *Rise up Singing: The Group Singing Songbook.*

- "Magic Penny," by Malvina Reynolds, p. 240 in *Rise up Singing: The Group Singing Songbook.*

- "Money (That's What I Want)," words and music by Berry Gordy, Jr. and Janie Bradford, p. 98 in *The Beatles: The First Four Albums From the Original British Collection.*

This can also be found in *The Complete Beatles Volume II* (Milwaukee, WI: Hal Leonard, 1988), p. 112.

- "Money, Money," words by Fred Ebb and music by John Kander (from the film *Cabaret*), p. 16 in *Cabaret* (vocal selections). Milwaukee, WI: Hal Leonard, 1972.

- "Pennies from Heaven," words by John Burke and music by Arthur Johnston, p. 144 in *The Decade Series: Songs of the 30's.* Milwaukee, WI: Hal Leonard, 1989.

  This can also be found in *Jazz Standards: 100 Great Jazz Favorites* (Milwaukee, WI: Hal Leonard, n.d.), p. 185.

- "Sing a Song of Sixpence" (traditional), p. 222 in *The Reader's Digest Children's Songbook,* edited by William L. Simon. Pleasantville, NY: Reader's Digest Association, 1985.

- "Taxman," words and music by George Harrison, p. 273 in *The Complete Beatles Volume II.*

- "We're in the Money (The Gold Diggers' Song)," words by Al Dubin and music by Harry Warren (from the film *Gold Diggers of 1933,* and from the musical *42nd Street*), p. 36 in *42nd Street—The Broadway Musical* (vocal selections). n.p.: Warner Brothers Publications, 1980.

  This can also be found in *Hollywood Musicals Year by Year: 1927–1939* (Milwaukee, WI: Hal Leonard, 1995), p. 47.

- "Who Wants to be a Millionaire?," words and music by Cole Porter (from the film *High Society*), p. 24 in *Hollywood Musicals Year by Year: 1956–1964.* Milwaukee, WI: Hal Leonard, 1995.

Most of these songs have been recorded.

MAGAZINES

- *Freebies*
  1135 Eugenia Place
  Box 5025
  Carpinteria, CA 93014-5025
  (805) 566-1225

- *Zillions*
  Consumers Union of the United States, Inc.
  101 Truman Avenue
  Yonkers, NY 10703-1057
  (914) 378-2000; subscriptions: (800) 234-1645

POETRY

Have your class chant this anonymous poem before starting their lesson on money:

"One for the Money"

One for the money
Two for the show
Three to get ready
Four—Let's go!

- "Baloney Belly Billy," p. 134 in *The New Kid on the Block,* by Jack Prelutsky, illustrated by James Stevenson. New York: Greenwillow, 1984.

- "The Coin," by Sara Teasdale, p. 138 in *The Arbuthnot Anthology of Children's Literature* (4th ed., rev.), selected by May Hill Arbuthnot, Dorothy M. Broderick, Shelton L. Root, Jr., Mark Taylor, and Evelyn L. Wenzel, illustrated by various artists. New York: Lothrop, Lee & Shepard, 1976.

- "The Dream," p. 18 in *Auntie's Knitting a Baby,* by Lois Simmie, illustrated by Anne Simmie. New York: Orchard, 1984.

- "Fantasy of an African Boy," by James Berry, p. 149 in *A New Treasury of Poetry,* compiled by Neil Philip, illustrated by John Lawrence. New York: Stewart, Tabori & Chang, 1990.

- "For Sale," p. 52 in *Where the Sidewalk Ends,* by Shel Silverstein, illustrated by the author. New York: Harper & Row, 1974.

- "The Googies are Coming," p. 50 in *Where the Sidewalk Ends.*

- "I Had But Fifty Cents," by Anonymous, p. 50 in *And the Green Grass Grew All Around: Folk Poetry from Everyone,* compiled by

Alvin Schwartz, illustrated by Sue Truesdell (New York: Harper-Collins, 1992).

A different version can be found in *For Laughing Out Loud: Poems to Tickle Your Funnybone,* selected by Jack Prelutsky, illustrated by Marjorie Priceman (New York: Knopf, 1991), p. 31.

- "If I Find a Penny," p. 3 in *The Butterfly Jar,* by Jeff Moss, illustrated by Chris Demarest. New York: Bantam, 1989.

- "It's a Bit Rich," by Max Fatchen, p. 29 in *The Oxford Treasury of Children's Poems,* selected by Michael Harrison and Christopher Stuart-Clark. Oxford: Oxford University Press, 1988.

- "Lunch Money," p. 7 in *Lunch Money and Other Poems About School,* by Carol Diggory Shields, illustrated by Paul Meisel. New York: Dutton Children's Books, 1995.

- "Money Box," p. 69 in *Quick, Let's Get Out of Here,* by Michael Rosen, illustrated by Quentin Blake. London: Andre Deutsch, 1983.

- "News Story," by William Cole, p. 33 in *For Laughing Out Loud: Poems to Tickle Your Funnybone.*

- "A Poem for a Pickle," in *A Poem for a Pickle: Funnybone Verses,* by Eve Merriam, illustrated by Sheila Hamanaka. New York: Morrow Junior Books, 1989.

- "A Rhyme," p. 42 in *The Other Side of the Door,* by Jeff Moss, illustrated by Chris Demarest. New York: Bantam, 1991.

- "The Silver Penny," by Walter De la Mare, p. 222 in *A New Treasury of Poetry.*

- * "Smart," by Shel Silverstein, p. 157 in *The Random House Book of Poetry for Children,* selected by Jack Prelutsky, illustrated by Arnold Lobel. New York: Random House, 1983.

   This is also found in *Where the Sidewalk Ends,* p. 35.

- "Song for Joey," by Michael Dennis Browne, p. 47 in *Oh, That's Ridiculous,* selected by William Cole, illustrated by Tomi Ungerer. New York: Viking, 1972.

A RIDDLE

- "Whoever makes it, tells it not," p. 45 in *From Sea to Shining Sea: A Treasury of American Folklore and Folk Songs,* compiled by Amy L. Cohn, illustrated by various renown artists. New York: Scholastic, 1993.

STORIES ABOUT MONEY

- * "The Great Manhattan Swindle," pp. 142–143 in *Destiny,* by Paul Aurandt. New York: Morrow, 1983.

- "£1,000,000 Bank-Note," pp. 315–332 in *The Complete Short Stories of Mark Twain,* edited by Charles Neider. Garden City, NY: Doubleday, 1985.

The following stories are found in *Chicken Soup for the Soul: 101 Stories to Open the Heart & Rekindle the Spirit,* written and compiled by Jack Canfield and Mark Victor Hansen (Deerfield Beach, FL: Health Communications, 1993):

- "Ask, Ask, Ask," by Jack Canfield and Mark V. Hansen, pp. 168–170

- "Tommy's Bumper Sticker," by Mark V. Hansen, pp. 173–177

The following stories were written by O. Henry and are found in *O. Henry Stories* (New York: Platt & Munk, 1962):

- "A Call Loan," pp. 241–249

- "Friends in San Rosario," pp. 315–336

- "The Gift of the Magi," pp. 40–48

- "Mammon and the Archer," pp. 374–383

- "One Dollar's Worth," pp. 67–77

- "The Ransom of Mack," pp. 454–463

- "The Ransom of Red Chief," pp. 13–29

The following tales based on the Midas legend are found in *The Arbuthnot Anthology of Children's Literature* (4th ed., rev.), selected by May Hill Arbuthnot, Dorothy M. Broderick, Shelton L. Root, Jr.,

Mark Taylor, and Evelyn L. Wenzel, illustrated by various artists. New York: Lothrop, Lee & Shepard, 1976:

- "The Golden Touch," by Nathaniel Hawthorne, pp. 440–446

- "Midas," retold by Thomas Bulfinch, pp. 439–440

The following tales about gold are found in *From Sea to Shining Sea: A Treasury of American Folklore and Folk Songs,* compiled by Amy L. Cohn, illustrated by various renown artists. New York: Scholastic, 1993.

- "The Mezcla Man," retold by J. Frank Dobie, pp. 30–32

- "The Raven and the Star Fruit Tree" (a Vietnamese folktale), retold by Tran Van Dien and Winabelle Gritter, pp. 368–369

RELATED BOOKS

Fiction

- Ada, Alma Flor. *The Gold Coin,* translated by Bernice Randall, illustrated by Neil Waldman. New York: Atheneum, 1991. **PJ**

  Trying to steal an old woman's gold coin, a thief follows her around the countryside and becomes involved in activities that eventually change his life.

- * Axelrod, Amy. *Pigs Will Be Pigs,* illustrated by Sharon McGinley-Nally. New York: Simon & Schuster Books for Young Readers, 1994. **PJ**

  A pig family turns the house upside-down looking for money to buy dinner at a restaurant.

- Banks, Jacqueline Turner. *Project Wheels.* Boston: Houghton Mifflin, 1993. **J**

  A young girl's relationship with her friends changes when she tries to raise money to buy a classmate a motorized wheelchair.

- Berenstain, Stan, and Jan Berenstain. *The Berenstain Bears' Trouble With Money,* illustrated by the authors. New York: Random House, 1983. **PJ**

  Brother Bear and Sister Bear learn important lessons about earning and spending money.

- Bethancourt, T. Ernesto. *The Me Inside of Me.* Minneapolis: Lerner, 1985. **YA**

  When 17-year-old Alfredo Flores inherits a lot of money after his parents die, he discovers being wealthy creates a new set of problems.

- Birdsye, Tom. *Tarantula Shoes.* New York: Holiday House, 1995. **J**

  See Program Plan II.

- Brittain, Bill. *All the Money in the World,* illustrated by Charles Robinson. New York: HarperTrophy, 1979. **J**

  Trouble follows when a young boy gets his wish for all the money in the world.

- Danziger, Paula. *Not for a Billion Gazillion Dollars.* New York: Delacorte, 1992. **J**

  Trying to earn enough money in order to buy a computer program, Matthew learns about the importance of money and eventually starts his own business.

- Fleischman, Sid. *The Ghost on Saturday Night,* illustrated by Eric Von Schmidt. Boston: Atlantic Monthly Press/Little, Brown, 1974. **J**

  A thick fog and a ghost-raising leads to more reward than Opie counted on.

- Giff, Patricia Reilly. *Count Your Money with the Polk Street School,* illustrated by Blanche Sims. New York: Yearling, 1994. **PJ**

  Ms. Rooney's class learns about money and saving when they try to earn enough money for a class trip. The book includes ideas for activities.

- Glaser, Linda. *Tanya's Big Green Dream,* illustrated by Susan McGinnis. New York: Macmillan, 1994. **J**

  See Program Plan I.

- Greenwald, Sheila. *The Mariah Delany Lending Library Disaster,* illustrated by the author. Boston: Houghton Mifflin, 1977. **J**

  An 11-year-old girl creates her own lending library in competition with the New York Public Library.

- Hautzig, Esther. *Riches,* illustrated by Donna Diamond. New York: Charlotte Zolotow/HarperCollins, 1992. **J+**

  Following the advice of a wise rabbi, a rich storekeeper discovers that giving of himself is better than just giving money.

- Herman, Charlotte. *Max Malone Makes a Million,* illustrated by Cat Bowman Smith. New York: Redfeather/Henry Holt, 1991. **J**

  Two boys are continually frustrated in their efforts to become rich, while their little neighbor makes money at whatever he attempts.

- Hoban, Lillian. *Arthur's Funny Money,* illustrated by the author. New York: Harper Trophy/ Harper & Row, 1981. **PJ**

  When Violet has a numbers problem and Arthur has no money, they go into business and solve both of their problems.

- Jones, Rebecca C. *Germy Blew the Bugle.* New York: Arcade/Little, Brown, 1990. **J**

  See Program Plan III.

- Kehret, Peg. *The Richest Kids in Town.* New York: Cobblehill Books/Dutton, 1994. **J**

  A new boy in town teams up with a classmate to earn money for a trip to his old neighborhood, but all their money-making schemes have unexpected results.

- Kent, Jack. *Piggy Bank Gonzales,* illustrated by the author. New York: Parents' Magazine Press, 1978. **PJ**

  A piggy bank, bored with his life, finds that life outside his Mexican town is too exciting.

- Manes, Stephen. *Make Four Million Dollars by Next Thursday!,* illustrated by George Ulrich. New York: Bantam Skylark, 1991. **J**

  A young boy attracts too much attention when he follows the zany advice from a "how-to-get-rich" book.

- Martin, Ann M. *The Baby-Sitters Club* series. New York: Scholastic. **J**

  Friends form a baby-sitting service in order to earn money.

- Mathis, Sharon Bell. *The Hundred Penny Box,* illustrated by Leo and Diane Dillon. New York: Viking, 1975. **J**

  Michael, whose great-great-great aunt lives with his family, tries to stop his mother from throwing out the elderly woman's old belongings.

- Mills, Claudia. *Cally's Enterprise.* New York: Macmillan, 1988. **J**

  Feeling pressured by overachieving parents and swept away by her new friend's money-making schemes, Cally tries to meet everyone's expectations but her own.

- Marzollo, Jean. *Slam Dunk Saturday,* illustrated by Blanche Sims. New York: Stepping Stone/Random House, 1994. **J**

  See Program Plan II.

- Pfeffer, Susan Beth. *Sara Kate, Superkid,* illustrated by Suzanne Hankins. New York: Redfeather/Henry Holt, 1994. **J**

  See Program Plan II.

- Quattlebaum, Mary. *Jackson Jones and the Puddle of Thorns,* illustrated by Melody Rosales. New York: Delacorte, 1994. **J**

  See Program Plan II.

- Robertson, Keith. *Henry Reed, Inc.,* illustrated by Robert McCloskey. New York: Viking, 1958. **J**

  During summer vacation, Henry and his friend Midge become involved in unusually profitable projects.

- Robertson, Keith. *Henry Reed's Baby-Sitting Service,* illustrated by Robert McCloskey. New York: Viking, 1966. **J**

  Henry and his partner Midge start a baby-sitting service and find a disappearing child and a peacock among their charges.

- Rockwell, Thomas. *How to Get Fabulously Rich,* illustrated by Anne Canevari Green. New York: Franklin Watts, 1990. **J**

  Billy has problems with his friends after winning money in the lottery.

- Sharmat, Marjorie Weinman. *Get Rich Mitch!,* illustrated by Loretta Lustig. New York: Morrow, 1985. **J**

After winning the sweepstakes, Mitch finds being a celebrity can have its shortcomings. This is a sequel to *Rich Mitch*.

- Sharmat, Marjorie Weinman. *Rich Mitch,* illustrated by Loretta Lustig. New York: Morrow, 1983. **J**

  Mitch's life becomes complicated after winning money in the sweepstakes.

- Spinelli, Jerry. *The Bathwater Gang Gets Down to Business,* illustrated by Meredith Johnson. Boston: Little, Brown, 1992. **J**

  Bertie comes up with a dishonest way to make his gang's pet-washing business a success.

- Spinelli, Jerry. *Dump Days.* Boston: Little, Brown, 1988. **J**

  Friends decide to have a perfect day before summer vacation ends.

- Stevens, Carla. *Lily and Miss Liberty,* illustrated by Deborah Kogan Ray. New York: Scholastic, 1992. **J**

  A little girl makes Miss Liberty crowns in order to help raise money for the statue's pedestal.

- Stewart, Sarah. *The Money Tree,* illustrated by David Small. New York: Farrar Straus Giroux, 1991. **PJ+**

  A money tree grows in Miss McGillicuddy's yard. She shares the bounty with a few children; however, there is soon an invasion of grown-ups motivated by greed.

- Wilson, Johnniece Marshall. *Poor Girl, Rich Girl.* New York: Scholastic, 1992. **J+**

  Miranda tries to earn money in order to buy contact lenses so that she can look beautiful.

Nonfiction/Informational

Most of these books include information about the history of money and banking, terminology, the banking system, career guidance, how to budget money, how to earn money, and numismatics.

- Adams, Barbara Johnston. *The Go-Around Dollar,* illustrated by Joyce Audy Zarins. New York: Four Winds, 1992. **PJ**

- Adler, David A. *All Kinds of Money,* illustrated by Tom Huffman. New York: Franklin Watts, 1984. **J**

- Arnold, Oren. *Marvels of the U.S. Mint,* photographs from various sources. New York: Abelard-Schuman, 1972. **J**

- Banks, Ann. *It's My Money: A Kid's Guide to the Green Stuff,* illustrated by Susan Natti. New York: Puffin, 1993. **J**

- Barkin, Carol, and Elizabeth James. *Jobs for Kids: The Guide to Having Fun and Making Money,* illustrated by Roy Doty. New York: Lothrop, Lee & Shepard, 1990. **J+**

- Berg, Adriane G., and Arthur Berg Bochner. *The Totally Awesome Money Book for Kids and Their Parents.* New York: Newmarket, 1993. **J+**

- Berry, Joy. *Every Kid's Guide to Making and Managing Money,* illustrated by Laurie Westdahl et al. Sebastopol, CA: Living Skills, 1986. **J**

- Cantwell, Lois. *Money and Banking,* photographs from various sources. New York: Franklin Watts, 1984. **J**

- Cribb, Joe. *Money,* illustrated by and photographs from various sources. New York: Knopf, 1990. **J**

- Davis, Mary. *Careers in a Bank,* photographs by Milton J. Blumenfeld. Minneapolis: Lerner, 1975. **J**

- Drew, Bonnie, and Noel Drew. *Fast Cash for Kids.* Franklin Lakes, NJ: Career Press, 1995. **J+**

- Elkin, Benjamin. *Money,* photographs from various sources. Chicago: Childrens Press, 1983. **J**

- Erlbach, Arlene. *The Kids' Business Book,* photographs by Jim Simondet and Nancy Smedstad. Minneapolis: Lerner, 1998. **J**

- Godfrey, Neale S. *Neale S. Godfrey's Ultimate Kids' Money Book,* illustrated by Randy Verougstraete. New York: Simon & Schuster Books for Young Readers, 1998. **J+**

- Gross, Ruth Belov. *Money, Money, Money,* illustrated by Leslie Jacobs. New York: Four Winds Press, 1971. **J**

- Haddock, Patricia. *Careers in Banking and Finance,* photographs from various sources. New York: Rosen, 1990. **YA**

- James, Elizabeth, and Carol Barkin. *Understanding Money,* illustrated by Santos Paniagua. Milwaukee: Raintree, 1977. **J**

- Johnson, Anne Akers. *The Buck Book: All Sorts of Things to Do with a Dollar Bill—Besides Spend It,* illustrated by John Craig, Ellery Knight, and Elizabeth Buchman. Palo Alto, CA: Klutz, 1993. **J**

- Kyte, Kathy S. *The Kids' Complete Guide to Money,* illustrated by Richard Brown. New York: Knopf, 1984. **J**

- Lewis, Brenda Ralph. *Coins & Currency,* illustrated by and photographs from various sources. New York: Random House, 1993. **J+**

- Maestro, Betsy. *The Story of Money,* illustrated by Giulio Maestro. New York: Clarion, 1993. **J**

- Mitgutsch, Ali. *From Gold to Money,* illustrated by the author. Minneapolis: Carolrhoda, 1985. **PJ**

- Nathan, Amy. *The Kids' Allowance Book,* illustrated by Debbie Palen. New York: Walker, 1998. **PJ**

- Otfinoski, Steve. *The Kids' Guide to Money: Earning It, Saving It, Spending It, Growing It, Sharing It,* illustrated by Kelly Kennedy. New York: Scholastic, 1996. **J+**

- Parker, Nancy Winslow. *Money, Money, Money: The Meaning of the Art and Symbols on United States Paper Currency,* illustrated by the author. New York: HarperCollins, 1995. **J**

- Rendon, Marion B., and Rachel Kranz. *Straight Talk About Money.* New York: Facts on File, 1992. **YA**

- Schwartz, David M. *If You Made a Million,* illustrated by Steven Kellogg. New York: Lothrop, Lee & Shepard, 1989. **PJ**

- Scott, Elaine. *The Banking Book,* illustrated by Kathie Abrams. New York: Frederick Warne, 1981. **YA**

- Wallace, G. David. *Money Basics,* illustrated by Janet D'Amato, photographs from various sources. Englewood Cliffs, NJ: Prentice-Hall, 1984. **J**

- Wilkinson, Elizabeth. *Making Cents: Every Kid's Guide to Money,* illustrated by Martha Weston. Boston: Little, Brown, 1989. **J**

- Wilt, Joy. *A Kid's Guide to Managing Money,* illustrated by Ernie Hergenroeder. Chicago: Childrens Press, 1979. **J**

Program IV Plan

GUEST READER

Journalist.

HOW TO FIND THE GUEST READER

- Call your local radio or television station news organization or your local newspaper. If you prefer, send a written invitation and then follow up with a telephone call. Find the numbers in the telephone directory. In addition, you can sometimes find the newspaper's address and telephone number in the paper's masthead (the box usually located near the front of the paper listing the people who work at the paper and their jobs).

- Contact the journalism department of your local college or university.

- Contact the Society of Professional Journalists for a possible referral:

Society of Professional Journalists
16 S. Jackson Street
Greencastle, IN 46135
(765) 653-3333

ESTIMATED TIME

30–45 minutes.

READ-ALOUD BOOK

The True Story of the 3 Little Pigs by A. Wolf, by Jon Scieszka, illustrated by Lane Smith. New York: Viking, 1989.

Remember the tale of the 3 little pigs? Well, you don't know the whole story. The wolf simply got a bad rap—all because the news media sensationalized the story and did not report the event objectively. A. Wolf sets us straight in this very funny book.

As an alternative read-aloud, the reporter can read an article or news story he wrote. (One of my Guest Readers, Christine Lund, anchor for KABC-TV local news, read the book suggested above. Another Guest Reader, Ron Latimore, editor of our community paper, *The Acorn,* read an article he wrote about an incident involving a racially motivated attack on a local family that occurred a few years before. The article tied in with the class's unit on prejudice and discrimination. Furthermore, the students were preparing to write reports on this topic. Mr. Latimore's talk gave them additional insight on how to conduct research.)

BEFORE THE VISIT

- If a radio or television reporter is the Guest Reader, decorate the bulletin board with a cut-out of a radio or TV set. Insert the local station's logo or a photo of the reporter in the center of the radio or TV set. (Ask the radio or TV station for publicity photos of the Guest Reader.)
- If the Guest Reader is with a newspaper, display articles from the paper. Alternative idea: Display a map of the United States or of the world. Surround the map with articles covering stories from different geographical settings. Draw a line from the article to its corresponding location on the map.

INTRODUCTION OF THE GUEST READER

"If you want to know what is happening in our community [the state, the country, the world!], the best paper/radio/TV news to read/to listen to/ to watch is (name of paper or radio/TV call-letters, and title of news program). We are fortunate to have as our Guest Reader, (title) from (organization), (Guest Reader's name)."

Guest Reader's Introduction of the Book

"We all *think* we know the tale of the 3 little pigs. But according to A. Wolf, the news media reported the story inaccurately. Mr. Wolf tells us *his* side of the story in this book, *The True Story of the 3 Little Pigs by A. Wolf.*"

Discussion Topics

Suggest to the Guest Reader to:

- Explain that a news article should provide the essential information: Who, What, Where, When, Why (journalism's five "W's"). When appropriate, an "H" for How and an "S" for Significance are added.

- Explain that good journalism should be fair, objective, and accurate. A reporter's opinion should not appear in his report. (Read examples of biased reporting.)

- Describe how a reporter checks the facts. A reporter researches the background of the topic by checking reference books, documents, and other articles written on the subject. A reporter also interviews many people.

- Explain the difference between a columnist's story, commentary, and editorial (where opinion is allowed) and a news article. (The TV anchor/reporter should explain the difference between a commentator and a reporter.)

- Explain the two meanings of the word "tabloid" (a small paper as opposed to a broadsheet and a paper or TV show with sensational news). Describe the difference between tabloid papers (and TV shows) such as the *National Enquirer,* magazines (especially those with a point of view), and newspapers/newscasts.

- Explain the difference between a feature story and a news story.

- Explain the importance of freedom of the press and why it is part of the Bill of Rights.

- Briefly describe a typical day on the job. Provide information about other positions on the staff and how these people help produce the newspaper/newscast. Try to include terms such as editor, assignment editor, wire service, deadline, lead story. If he has done any investigative reporting, describe what that was like.

- Use visual aids. For example, a TV anchor/reporter could show the class a script of a newscast.

- Give a brief history of newspapers:

  –the first news sheet was handwritten in Rome in 500 B.C. and posted for the public to see

  –in many parts of the world, the news was reported by people who traveled from town to town telling the news in songs and poems. (Suggest students read *Adam of the Road* by Elizabeth Janet Gray, which describes a minstrel's life in the Middle Ages)

  –the first printed newspaper was made in China in the eighth century. It was printed by hand, using wooden blocks

  –in the 1440s the printing press was invented in Germany by Johann Gutenberg. Now presses could be used to print many copies of a newspaper

  –some consider an early form of a *real* newspaper to be the *London Gazette,* published in 1666. The first daily paper, the *Daily Courant,* was printed in London in 1702

  –the first newspapers in the American colonies were printed in Boston. However, the first daily in the United States was *The Pennsylvania Evening Post and Daily Advertiser,* printed in Philadelphia in 1783

  –the first inexpensive American newspaper, the penny newspaper, was the *New York Sun,* started in 1833. More people were able to afford to buy a paper. Penny newspapers were similar to today's newspapers

KIDS' ACTIVITIES

Ask the students to:

- Learn terminology such as editor (including copy editor, city editor, assignment editor), editorial, op-ed, wire services (including the Associated Press, United Press International, and Reuters), lead, feature, beat, circulation, classifieds, box score, scoop, tip, graphic, "putting the paper to bed," television news anchor, teleprompter, sound bite, updates, voice-over. Create word puzzles using these terms.

- Create a poster identifying the parts of a newspaper such as flag, masthead, headline, subhead, dateline, byline, sidebar, and the different sections of the paper such as sports, entertainment, weather, metro news.

- Conduct an article/ item search. Find clippings with the content described below. Ask the students to summarize the content of each article or clipping in their own words. For news articles, or any appropriate item, students should use the five W's of journalism: Who What, Where, When, Why (and sometimes How and Significance) in their summaries. The reports should include a copy of the actual clip and a notation of the newspaper, date, section, and page number where the item was found. (This exercise provides an opportunity for the students to explore and learn about the different sections of the newspaper.)

  –a story with a dateline from a French-speaking country. (Variation: Find an article about any foreign locale. Locate the area on a map)

  –information regarding the weather forecast for another city

  –a story about a scientific discovery that will change the future

  –a story about an animal

  –a story about a local sports event

  –a story about a child

  –a story about the state government

  –a story about the President or his family

  –a story about a local business

  –information that will help the reader plan a trip

  –information that will help the reader find a job

  –information that will help the reader find a used car

  –information that will help the reader plan a weekend

  –information that will help the reader find a sale on clothes

  –a humorous story

  –a positive, upbeat story

–a comic strip that is funny. (Explain why this particular comic tickled them)

–a story that provides a recipe or gives information about nutrition

–an item with gossip about a celebrity

–a photo of a tragic event

–a story about a religious event

–a local person's obituary

–an item that shows the author's opinion on an issue

–a story about a conflict based on ethnic or religious differences

- Create a collage of newspaper headlines or articles expressing a point of view, such as the senselessness of war, or a theme, such as examples of "happy" news.

- Write a report or create a timeline of the history of newspapers and broadcast journalism. Variation: Cover the history of news reporting (and changing standards of reporting) in America only. Remember to include information about "yellow journalism" and "muckrakers."

- Present skits or "living tableaux" with narration to show a brief history of the news. (*Note:* Teachers can assign groups to represent one event in the history of news reporting. Each group performs its skit for the class.) Read books such as *Behind the Headlines: The Story of American Newspapers* by Thomas Fleming, *Deadline! From News to Newspapers* by Gail Gibbons, and *Newspapers* by David Petersen, for information.

- Write reports about prominent news people such as Horace Greeley, William Randolph Hearst, Joseph Pulitzer, Lincoln Steffens, Nellie Bly, Ida B. Wells, Ernie Pyle, or Edward R. Murrow. Include current journalists as well. Variation: Present skits representing episodes from these people's lives or tell their stories in the first person. Dress in costume.

- Freedom of the Press is part of the Bill of Rights. John Peter Zenger's case in 1735 was the first prominent battle for freedom of the press in America. Read about Zenger in books such as *Behind the Headlines: The Story of American Newspapers* by Thomas Fleming; *Taking on the Press: Constitutional Rights in Conflict* by

Melvyn Bernard Zerman; and a fictional account, *The Printer's Apprentice* by Stephen Krensky. Stage a mock trial of this case. Does the student jury come up with a different verdict?

- Although there is freedom of the press, news people are expected to follow a code of ethics, which includes writing accurate reports, giving accused people an opportunity to respond, not abusing the journalistic role for selfish reasons, avoiding conflicts of interest, resisting pressure from special interest groups to write stories favorable to that group, or not to cover a news item because it may be unfavorable to the group. Journalism ethics is covered in books such as *What's New, Lincoln?* by Dale Fife; *Germy Blew the Bugle* by Rebecca C. Jones; *The Ninth Issue* by Dallin Malmgren; *The Yellow Line* by Ernie Rydberg; *Megan's Beat* by Lou Willett Stanek; and nonfiction books such as *How to Write a News Article* by Michael Kronenwetter; *Journalism Ethics* by Michael Kronenwetter; and *Taking on the Press: Constitutional Rights in Conflict* by Melvyn Bernard Zerman. Discuss with class-mates ideas presented in these books and cite examples of real-life journalists who have crossed ethical lines.

- Critics accuse the press of slanting the news, invading privacy, destroying people's reputations, giving away military secrets, get-ting information in underhanded ways, sensationalizing the news in order to sell more papers (or to get higher ratings). Write an essay agreeing or disagreeing with the critics. Are abuses wide-spread or rare? Remember to present examples to back-up the viewpoint. The books by Kronenwetter and Zerman and *The Berenstain Bears and the School Scandal Sheet* by Stan and Jan Berenstain, *Karen's Newspaper* by Ann M. Martin, *Bright Days, Stupid Nights* by Norma Fox Mazer and Harry Mazer, and *I Hate My Hero* by Jacqueline Shannon discuss these issues.

- Find a straight news article where the writer's bias has slipped into the story. This can happen through the facts and details the writer decided to use or omit, or through the writer's choice of verbs and adjectives. For examples of this, read *How to Write a News Article* by Michael Kronenwetter.

- According to the book, *Journalism Ethics* by Michael Kronen-wetter, when journalists report the news they must keep their opinion and bias out of the article; when they analyze or explain the facts, journalists are freer to express their opinions but in a balanced way. When they are editorializing, journalists are free to express their viewpoint. Compare and contrast examples of news articles, analytical reports, columns, and editorials.

- Find an example of an editorial or commentary. Write an essay agreeing or disagreeing with the author's opinion. In addition, listen to a talk-radio host. Describe his viewpoints and write an essay agreeing or disagreeing with his stance. Remember to use critical thinking when analyzing the editorial or commentary.

- Write an editorial about an important issue.

- Write a letter to the editor about an important issue.

- Find an example of a political cartoon. Write an essay agreeing or disagreeing with the cartoonist's viewpoint.

- Create a political cartoon.

- Write a report about the history of political cartoons. Include information about Thomas Nast.

- Because of space or time limitations, a story may not be fully covered, thus impacting a reader's/viewer's perception. Find examples of this and share them with classmates.

- Find articles from different newspapers (or reports from radio/TV news programs on different channels) covering the same story. Compare and contrast the treatments of this one story.

- Compare and contrast the treatment of one story as covered by television and radio newscasts, news magazines, and newspapers.

- Television techniques can impact the way a viewer perceives a story. For instance, a TV interviewer's facial expression or tone of voice when asking questions could influence the way the viewer thinks about the person being interviewed. Find examples and discuss with classmates.

- An editor once said, "When a dog bites a man, that's not news. But when a man bites a dog, that's news." Does the press give a full picture of daily events, or do we get a skewed perception because the press usually only covers the unusual? Discuss this issue with classmates. This topic is examined in the book *How Do You Know It's True? Sifting Sense From Nonsense* by David Klein and Marymae E. Klein (New York: Scribner's, 1984).

- The American Society of Newspaper Editors stated that the role of the press is not just to inform or to serve as a forum for debate, but also to scrutinize the forces of power in society, including the government. Cite examples, past and present, where the press has fulfilled this role.

- Discuss why the press is called the "Fourth Estate."

- Write a report about ways the press impacted events in history, such as Watergate or the Spanish-American War. In addition, discuss with classmates how the press impacts American politics (see **VIDEOS**).

- In the books *What's New, Lincoln?*, by Dale Fife, and *The Yellow Line*, by Ernie Rydberg, reporters solve crimes. Write a report about instances where real-life journalists helped solve or helped uncover a crime. *Behind the Headlines: The Story of American Newspapers* by Thomas Fleming and *Taking on the Press: Constitutional Rights in Conflict* by Melvyn Bernard Zerman discuss a few past cases.

- Discuss the difference between libel (defamation of character in printing and writing) and slander (defamation in speech). There have been a number of cases where people have sued the press for libel, such as Carol Burnett's suit against the *National Enquirer*. Debate these cases with classmates. Find information in books such as *Journalism Ethics* by Michael Kronenwetter and *Taking on the Press: Constitutional Rights in Conflict* by Melvyn Bernard Zerman.

- There are a number of cases where the government has tried to censor the press, including the Sedition Act of 1798, and in 1971, when the federal government tried to stop *The New York Times* from publishing excerpts of the Pentagon Papers. Study a few of these cases and debate each case with classmates. Read *Behind the Headlines: The Story of American Newspapers*, by Thomas Fleming, *Journalism Ethics*, by Michael Kronenwetter, and *Taking on the Press: Constitutional Rights in Conflict*, by Melvyn Bernard Zerman, for information.

- Discuss and debate freedom of the press for student publications, including underground newspapers. Read *The Berenstain Bears and the School Scandal Sheet* by Stan and Jan Berenstain and

Buffalo Brenda by Jill Pinkwater, two fictional accounts about student underground newspapers, and *Taking on the Press: Constitutional Rights in Conflict* by Melvyn Bernard Zerman, which describes the real-life case of Charlie Quarterman, who was suspended from his high school for distributing an underground newspaper. *The Ninth Issue* by Dallin Malmgren examines the issue of a school censoring the official school newspaper and mentions the case of *Hazelwood School District v. Kuhlmeier,* in which, in 1988, the Supreme Court ruled that teachers may censor the school newspaper (the case involved an article about student pregnancy).

- Discuss "shield laws" and debate the issue: should a reporter be able to conceal a source? Read the books by Kronenwetter and Zerman for a discussion of this issue.

- Should a journalist be able to go undercover in order to investigate a story? Discuss this with classmates.

- In *Dear Lovey Hart, I Am Desperate* by Ellen Conford, Carrie, an advice columnist for her school newspaper, discovers how difficult it is to solve problems. Read advice columns such as *Dear Abby* and write an essay that agrees or disagrees with her advice. Then write a response to the same question in their own words.

- It is important that, whenever possible, a reporter gets information from a primary source. For a good example of how facts can become otherwise distorted, read the first-level reader *Good News* by Barbara Brenner, illustrated by Kate Duke (New York: Bantam Little Rooster, 1991). In addition, play the "telephone game": Whisper a sentence into a player's ear. That player whispers the sentence into the next player's ear, thus continuing down the line of people. The last person who receives the message announces it to the group. More often than not, the sentence is entirely different than the original.

- In *Val McCall, Ace Reporter* by Fran Manushkin, Val's article is sabotaged. With no time to review her work, and therefore not knowing of the changes, she electronically sends her article to the newspaper's printing press. The sabotaged article appears in the paper the next day. Discuss if this is a realistic portrayal of newspaper operations.

- Do publications ever make errors? Cite examples of the past such as the *Chicago Daily Tribune* headline proclaiming "DEWEY DEFEATS TRUMAN." Discuss the recall of the *Special Newsweek Edition: Your Child* (Spring/Summer, 1997), because it included erroneous information. (On page 58, a 5-month-old baby was described as being able to hand-feed zwiebacks and raw carrot chunks to himself.) Find current examples of articles that include inaccurate information.

- With classmates, create a newspaper, magazine, or radio/television newscast. Include information on classroom or school events. (Variation: Each student chooses one event or topic to write about in a news article format. It could be about a family, community or school event. Read the article to the class.) Books such as *Make Your Own Newspaper* by Ray and Chris Harris, *How to Write a Newspaper Article* by Michael Kronenwetter, *The Furry News: How to Make a Newspaper* by Loreen Leedy, *Tell Me About Yourself: How to Interview Anyone from Your Friends to Famous People* by D. L. Mabery, *The Newspaper Anti-Coloring Book* by Susan Striker, and *Create Your Own Magazine* by Barbara Taylor offer ideas and guidelines.

- The books, *The Aztec News* by Philip Steele, illustrated by various artists (Cambridge, MA: Candlewick Press, 1997) and *The Egyptian News* by Scott Steedman, illustrated by various artists (Cambridge, MA: Candlewick Press, 1997), present the history of these peoples in the format of a newspaper, as if it were published in that time period. (The series also includes *The Greek News, The Roman News, The Stone Age News,* and *The Viking News.*) With classmates, create a newspaper, magazine, or radio/ television newscast as if it were taking place in a specific, historic time-period. Variation: Choose one historic event to report.

- Take a photo or draw a picture depicting an important event in the family, community, or school. Write a caption for the picture.

- Read reviews (art, music, film, television, book, restaurant) and write an essay agreeing or disagreeing with the review. Variation: Write an original review.

- Write a history about newspaper comic strips.

- Create a comic strip.

- Characters in the books *The Ninth Issue,* by Dallin Malmgren, *I Hate My Hero,* by Jacqueline Shannon, and *Megan's Beat,* by Lou Willett Stanek, find their relationships with their best friends changing. Write a story, poem, or essay about a friendship they had that changed for the best or for the worst. Variation: Write a feature article about the changing dynamics of friendship. Interview psychologists, teachers, and friends. Alternatively, write a feature about a special friendship.
- In *Paperboy* by Mary Kay Kroeger and Louise Borden, Willie's ability to sell papers is impacted by a sports-news event. In *I Hate My Hero* by Jacqueline Shannon, Rachel becomes the focus of a news story. Write a report about a news event that directly or indirectly affected students' lives; or, if they were the subject of a news item, write a report about that.
- In the book *Really Weird Stories,* the author, Dana Del Prado, fictionalizes stories based on stories in the news. Choose a real story from the news and write a fictionalized account of it. (It doesn't have to be a weird story!)
- Learn about careers in the news business. Choose one position that seems interesting and write a report describing the job. If possible, interview someone who has that job. Include the information in the report. Refer to **RELATED BOOKS** for materials that provide information on this topic.
- Create jewelry, puppets, masks, flowers, costumes, etc., using newspapers. For instructions on newspaper art projects, check out *Great Newspaper Crafts* by F. Virginia Walter (New York: A Sterling/Hyperion Book/Sterling Publishing, 1991).
- Have a "newspaper toss" contest. For example, who can throw the paper the farthest? Who can throw it the most accurately? (Toss it onto a designated area.) Variation: Create a "deliver the newspaper" obstacle course. Players carry a canvas bag filled with newspapers. Here are suggestions for stations:

    Station 1—fold newspapers

    Station 2—toss the paper onto a platform

    Station 3—toss the paper at a target with a bullseye

    Station 4—toss the paper at a target mounted high off the ground on a tall structure

Station 5—toss the paper into a box

Station 6—toss the paper over a wading pool of water or past an oscillating lawn sprinkler

Targets can be placed close to the player, far from the player, etc. If this is a competition, players can receive points for speed and accuracy.

Note to Teachers: Many newspapers sponsor a News in Education program that provides guidelines and activities for students. Contact your area's newspaper for information.

VIDEOS

Instructional Videos

• *How It's Done: From Roller Coaster to Ice Cream* (How It's Done, Inc./Video Treasures, 1995. 32 minutes)

Includes a segment with a behind-the-scenes look at how a TV news broadcast gets ready for prime time.

• *Illusions of News: The Public Mind with Bill Moyers* (Alvin H. Perlmutter, Inc., and Public Affairs Television Inc./PBS Video, 1989. 58 minutes)

Discusses the impact of visual images on news and politics and changing values in journalism. (This video is for mature students.)

Films on Video

• *All the President's Men,* starring Robert Redford, Dustin Hoffman, and Jason Robards (Warner Brothers Wildwood Enterprises, 1976/Warner Home Video, 1991. 139 minutes. Rated PG)

The film presents the real story of *The Washington Post's* journalists Carl Bernstein and Bob Woodward's investigation of Watergate. It is based on their book with the same title.

• *Citizen Kane,* starring Orson Welles, Joseph Cotten, and Agnes Moorehead (An RKO Radio Picture A Mercury Production, 1941/The Nostalgia Merchant, Fox Hills Video, 1986. 120 minutes. Not rated)

This classic film is a study of a powerful newspaper publisher. The character of Kane has often been compared to the real-life publisher, William Randolph Hearst.

- *The Front Page,* starring Walter Matthau, Jack Lemmon, Susan Sarandon, and Carol Burnett (Universal Pictures–A Billy Wilder Film, 1974/MCA Home Video, 1992. 105 minutes. Rated PG)

  Based on the play by Ben Hecht and Charles MacArthur, the film is a newspaper comedy set in the 1920's. This is a remake. Earlier versions include: *The Front Page* with Adolphe Menjou and Pat O'Brien, and *His Girl Friday* with Cary Grant and Rosalind Russell.

- *Newsies,* starring Robert Duvall and Ann-Margret (Walt Disney Pictures/Walt Disney Home Videos, 1992. 121 minutes. Rated PG)

  A Disney musical that is about a group of newsboys who fight an unscrupulous newspaper tycoon. The film is based on a true story. In 1899, New York City newsboys went on strike when Joseph Pulitzer threatened to reduce their profits by one-tenth of a cent.

SONGS

- "Baby June and Her Newsboys," words by Stephen Sondheim and music by Jule Styne, p. 45 in *Gypsy* (vocal score of the Broadway musical). n.p.: Williamson Music & Stratford Music/Chappell, 1960.

- "A Day in the Life," words and music by John Lennon and Paul McCartney, p. 134 in *The Complete Beatles Volume I.* Milwaukee, WI: Hal Leonard, 1988.

- "I Read It in the Daily News," words and music by Tom Paxton, p. 196 in *Songs That Changed the World,* edited by Wanda Willson Whitman. New York: Crown, 1969.

- "It's a Good News Week," words and music by Kenneth King, p. 106 in *50's & 60's Showstoppers.* Miami, FL: Warner Brothers, 1993.

- "Newspapermen," by Vern Partlow, p. 174 in *Carry It On! A History in Song and Picture of the Working Men and Women of*

America, by Pete Seeger and Bob Reiser. New York: Simon & Schuster, 1985.

• "Washington Post March," by John Philip Sousa, recorded on *Stars and Stripes Forever: Favorite Marches by Sousa and Other March Kings* (Andre Kostelanetz and His Orchestra)—CBS Records Odyssey (YT 38918).

Sousa was commissioned by Frank Hatton, one of the owners of the newspaper *The Washington Post,* to compose a march to be played at the ceremony the paper was sponsoring to honor student winners of an essay contest organized by the *Post's* Amateur Authors' Association. The march was premiered at the grounds of the Smithsonian Institution on June 15, 1889. When the national association of dance masters later used the piece to introduce a new dance, the two step, at their national convention, the "Washington Post March" became a hit in both America and Europe. Consequently, the newspaper received a lot of publicity and prominence. This piece was the beginning of a genre of marches associated with newspapers, one of the most recent being Leonard Smith's "Advocate-Messenger March" of 1990. Two CD's of newspaper marches performed by the Advocate Brass Band are available: *The "Washington Post" & Other American Newspaper Marches* and *The "Chicago Tribune": More American Newspaper Marches.* (There are many recordings of the "Washington Post March" by Sousa.)

MAGAZINES

The following magazines include articles about writing, but not necessarily journalism:

• *Authorship*
National Writer's Association
1450 S. Havana Street, Suite 424
Aurora, CO 80012
(303) 751-7844

• Canadian Authors Association
Box 419
Campbellford, ON K0L 1L0, Canada
(705) 653-0323

Look for websites that feature kids' writings (e.g., http://www. kidpub.org/kidpub/intro.html). There are also publications that print works by young people, such as:

- *Merlyn's Pen* (The National Magazines of Student Writing)
  P.O. Box 1058
  East Greenwich, RI 02818-0964
  (401) 885-5175

  (There are two editions: Intermediate Edition, geared to grades 6 thru 9, and Senior Edition, geared to grades 9 thru 12.)

For a list of additional publications, check out *The Market Guide for Young Writers: Where and How to Sell What You Write* by Kathy Henderson.

The following are publications that discuss current events and are geared towards young people :

- *Current Events* (Weekly Reader)
  245 Long Hill Road, Box 2791
  Middletown, CT 06457-9291
  (203) 638-2400

  Subscription:
  3000 Cindel Drive
  Delran, NJ 08075
  (800) 446-3355

- *Junior Scholastic*
  Scholastic, Inc.
  555 Broadway
  New York, NY 10012-3999
  (212) 343-6100 or (800) 325-6149

- *Time For Kids*
  Time, Inc.,
  Time & Life Building, Rockefeller Center
  1271 Avenue of the Americas
  New York, NY 10020-1393
  (212) 522-1212

POETRY

- "From Number Nine, Penwiper Mews," by Edward Gorey, p. 58 in *Lots of Limericks,* selected by Myra Cohn Livingston, illustrated by Rebecca Perry. New York: Macmillan, 1991.

- "The Morning Star," by Primus St. John, p. 346 in *The Poetry of Black America,* edited by Arnold Adoff. New York: Harper & Row, 1973.

- "The News," p. 109 in *The Best of Michael Rosen,* by Michael Rosen, illustrated by Quentin Blake. Berkeley, CA: Wetlands Press, 1995.

   This can also be found in *Spaceways: An Anthology of Space Poems,* selected by John Foster, illustrated by John Foster et al. (Oxford: Oxford University Press, 1986), p. 43.

- "News Brief," p. 11 in *A Pizza the Size of the Sun,* by Jack Prelutsky, illustrated by James Stevenson. New York: Greenwillow, 1996.

- "News Story," by William Cole, p. 33 in *For Laughing Out Loud: Poems to Tickle Your Funnybone,* selected by Jack Prelutsky, illustrated by Marjorie Priceman. New York: Knopf, 1991.

- "They Are Killing All the Young Men," by David Henderson, p. 414 in *The Poetry of Black America*

STORIES FROM NEWSPAPERS

The following stories with introductions by Jim Trelease are from the "Paper Clips" section (pp. 395–431) of the book, *Read All About It!: Great Read-Aloud Stories, Poems, & Newspaper Pieces for Preteens and Teens,* edited by Jim Trelease (New York: Penguin, 1993). The first four are good examples of works by columnists:

- * "Wrong Mom? Tough!," by Mike Royko, pp. 398–402

- * "Nothing To Worry About" and "The Turtle," by Jim Bishop, pp. 403–410

- * "He Was No Bum," by Bob Greene, pp. 411–416

- * "The Yellow Handkerchief," by Pete Hamill, pp. 417–423

The following two stories are good examples of op-ed pieces. Jim Trelease's introduction of these two works, "All the Views Fit to Print," provides an excellent history and description of the op-ed pages:

•* "I've Got Your Number," by Robe Imbriano, pp. 424–427

•* "Why Ali Loved Flag Burnings," by Craig Nelsen, pp. 428–431

RELATED BOOKS

Fiction

• Berenstain, Stan, and Jan Berenstain. *The Berenstain Bears and the School Scandal Sheet,* illustrated by the authors. New York: Big Chapter Book/Random House, 1994. **J**

Brother Bear and his friends start an underground newspaper at school and learn about freedom of the press and responsible journalism.

• Cleary, Beverly. *Henry and the Paper Route,* illustrated by Louis Darling. New York: Morrow, 1957. **J**

Henry has funny experiences trying to get a paper route.

• Conford, Ellen. *Dear Lovey Hart, I Am Desperate.* Boston: Little, Brown, 1975. **YA**

Carrie encounters more problems than she anticipated when she becomes an advice columnist for the school newspaper.

• Fife, Dale. *What's New, Lincoln?,* illustrated by Paul Galdone. New York: Coward-McCann, 1970. **J**

Lincoln gets into trouble with his neighbors when he starts a newspaper.

• Hall, Malcolm. *Deadlines,* illustrated by Bruce Degen. New York: Coward, McCann & Geoghegan, 1982. **PJ**

His friends at the paper try to help sports reporter Humphrey Snake type faster so he can meet his deadlines.

• Hall, Malcolm. *Forecast,* illustrated by Bruce Degen. New York: Coward, McCann & Geoghegan, 1977. **PJ**

Caroline Porcupine must prove that she can handle the job of weather reporter.

- Hall, Malcolm. *Headlines,* illustrated by Wallace Tripp. New York: Coward, McCann & Geoghegan, 1973. **PJ**

There are missing letters in Theodore Cat's newspaper office.

- Jones, Rebecca C. *Germy Blew the Bugle.* New York: Arcade/Little, Brown, 1990. **J**

Germy dreams of making a fortune with his newspaper but his plan backfires.

- Krensky, Stephen. *The Printer's Apprentice,* illustrated by Madeline Sorel. New York: Delacorte, 1995. **J**

In 1735 a young printer's apprentice learns about freedom of the press when Peter Zenger is arrested for criticizing the government.

- Kroeger, Mary Kay, and Louise Borden. *Paperboy,* illustrated by Ted Lewin. New York: Clarion, 1996. **PJ+**

In 1927 Cincinnati, a paperboy tries to sell "extras" on the Dempsey–Tunney fight.

- Malmgren, Dallin. *The Ninth Issue.* New York: Laurel Leaf/Dell, 1989. **YA**

A faculty advisor and the students on the school newspaper staff are in trouble with the school administration when they print articles on controversial topics.

- Manushkin, Fran. *Val McCall, Ace Reporter.* New York: Puffin, 1995. **J**

When a libelous story with her byline appears in her stepfather's newspaper, Val's guardian angel and her friends help find the person responsible.

- Martin, Ann M. *Karen's Newspaper* (Baby-Sitters Club Little Sister series, no. 40), illustrated by Susan Tang. New York: Scholastic, 1993. **J**

Karen and her friends learn about ethics in journalism when they print secrets about their neighbors in their newspaper.

- Mazer, Norma Fox, and Harry Mazer. *Bright Days, Stupid Nights.* New York: Bantam, 1992. **YA**

  During a summer internship on a newspaper, 14-year-old Vicki writes a sensational story about one of the other interns.

- Pilkey, Dav. *The Paperboy,* illustrated by the author. New York: Orchard, 1996. **PJ+**

  A paperboy and his dog enjoy the quiet of early morning while they make their deliveries.

- Pinkwater, Jill. *Buffalo Brenda.* New York: Aladdin/Simon & Schuster, 1989. **YA**

  Two friends start an underground newspaper in their high school and provide a live buffalo as a mascot for the football team.

- Prado, Dana Del. *Really Weird News Stories,* illustrated by M. Washington. New York: Kid Backs/Random House, 1996. **J**

  Fictionalized stories based on real news stories.

- Rydberg, Ernie. *The Yellow Line.* New York: Hawthorn, 1969. **J**

  When a teenage reporter untangles a mystery, small-town secrets are revealed.

- Shannon, Jacqueline. *I Hate My Hero.* New York: Simon & Schuster Books for Young Readers, 1992. **J**

  A young girl is excited to work with her best friend on the class's Video News hour until her friend saves her life and becomes a hero and a snob.

- Stanek, Lou Willett. *Megan's Beat.* New York: Dial Books for Young Readers/Dutton, 1983. **J**

  Megan's life becomes complicated when she writes a gossip column for the school newspaper.

Nonfiction/Informational

Most of these books include information about the history of journalism, terminology, journalism ethics, career guidance, creating a newspaper, writing hints, behind-the-scene looks at newspapers, and newscasts.

- Craig, Janet. *What's It Like to Be a . . . Newspaper Reporter,* illustrated by Richard Max Kolding. Mahwah, NJ: Troll, 1990. **J**

- English, Betty Lou. *Behind the Headlines at a Big City Paper,* photographs by the author. New York: Lothrop, Lee & Shepard, 1985. **J+**

- Fitz-Gerald, Christine Maloney. *I Can Be a Reporter,* photographs from various sources. Chicago: Childrens Press, 1986. **J**

- Fleming, Thomas. *Behind the Headlines: The Story of American Newspapers.* New York: Walker, 1989. **J+**

- Gibbons, Gail. *Deadline! From News to Newspaper,* illustrated by the author. New York: Crowell, 1987. **PJ**

- Hampton, Wilborn. *Kennedy Assassinated! The World Mourns: A Reporter's Story,* photographs from various sources. Cambridge, MA: Candlewick, 1997. **J+**

  The author's personal account of how he and other reporters covered this major event.

- Harris, Ray, and Chris Harris. *Make Your Own Newspaper.* Holbrook, MA: Bob Adams, 1993. **J**

- Hautzig, Esther. *On the Air: Behind the Scenes at a TV Newscast,* photographs by David Hautzig. New York: Macmillan, 1991. **J+**

- Henderson, Kathy. *The Market Guide for Young Writers: Where and How to Sell What You Write.* Cincinnati, OH: Writer's Digest, 1996. **J+**

- Jaspersohn, William. *A Day in the Life of a Television News Reporter,* photographs by the author. Boston: Little, Brown, 1981. **J**

- Jaspersohn, William. *Magazine: Behind the Scenes at* Sports Illustrated. Boston: Little, Brown, 1983. **YA**

- Koral, April. *In the Newsroom,* photographs by Carl Glassman. New York: A First Book/Franklin Watts, 1989. **J**

- Kronenwetter, Michael. *How to Write a News Article,* photographs from various sources. New York: Franklin Watts, 1995. **YA**

- Kronenwetter, Michael. *Journalism Ethics,* photographs from various sources. New York: Franklin Watts, 1988. **YA**

- •* Leedy, Loreen. *The Furry News: How to Make a Newspaper,* illustrated by the author. New York: Holiday House, 1990. **PJ**

- • Mabery, D. L. *Tell Me About Yourself: How to Interview Anyone from Your Friends To Famous People.* Minneapolis: Lerner, 1985. **J+**

- • Merbreier, W. Carter, with Linda Capus Riley. *Television: What's Behind What You See,* illustrated by Michael Chesworth. New York: Farrar, Straus and Giroux, 1996. **J**

- • Petersen, David. *Newspapers,* photographs from various sources. Chicago: Childrens Press, 1983. **PJ**

- • Striker, Susan. *The Newspaper Anti-Coloring Book.* New York: An Owl Book/Henry Holt, 1992. **J**

- • Taylor, Barbara. *Create Your Own Magazine,* illustrated by Brett Brandon. New York: Sterling, 1993. **J**

- • Wickenden, Martha T. *A Day in the Life of a Newspaper Reporter,* photographs by Michael Plunkett and Larry French. Mahwah, NJ: Troll, 1991. **J**

- • Zerman, Melvyn Bernard. *Taking on the Press: Constitutional Rights in Conflict,* photographs from various sources. New York: Crowell, 1986. **YA**

Program V Plan

GUEST READER

Historian (medieval period) or history re-enactors.

HOW TO FIND THE GUEST READER

- Call the local college or university's history department and ask them to recommend a professor or historian as Guest Reader.
- Contact the Society for Creative Anachronism, an educational organization dedicated to the research and re-creation of medieval and Renaissance culture, including the arts, sciences, combat, speech, dress, courtly manners—all areas of everyday life from noble to peasant. One of the Society's purposes is to teach others what they have learned, and therefore its members welcome opportunities to give school presentations. Ask the national headquarters to provide you with the address and telephone number for the chapter in your area. The national headquarters' address is:

  Society for Creative Anachronism, Inc.
  Office of the Registry, P.O. Box 360789
  Milpitas, CA 95036-0789
  (408) 263-9305, (408) 263-0641 (fax)

ESTIMATED TIME

One hour.

READ-ALOUD BOOK

Sir Gawain and the Loathly Damsel, retold by Joanna Troughton, illustrated by the author. New York: Dutton, 1972.

Adapted from an anonymous fifteenth-century poem, *The Weddynge of Sir Gawain and Dame Ragnell,* this is the tale of a hideous-looking lady who saves the life of King Arthur by answering the riddle: What is it in all the world that women most desire? In exchange for the answer, Sir Gawain, Arthur's best-loved knight, must agree to marry the loathly damsel. When he does, she is released from an evil enchantment and transforms into a beautiful woman. There are many versions of this story; however, Troughton's book is particularly suitable for reading to a large group. The story is deftly told and the illustrations are bold and colorful. Plus, in Troughton's story, Sir Gawain is depicted as much more gallant and kind than in other adaptations of the tale, including Selina Hasting's *Sir Gawain and the Loathly Lady.* However, in my opinion, the answer to the riddle is better stated by Hasting. In Troughton's book, the answer is "What woman wants is power over men." In Hasting's retelling, the answer is that "Woman desires to have her own way." Ironically, in the Middle Ages women rarely had any control over their destiny.

The Guest Reader will need to condense the story, and in the tradition of a minstrel, may also choose to tell it in his own words. As alternative readings, consider other legends or one of Chaucer's *Canterbury Tales* found in **RELATED BOOKS**. These stories will need to be shortened.

BEFORE THE VISIT

- If the Guest Readers are history re-enactors, ask them what kind of space they require. For example, if they are going to engage in mock combat, you may need to reserve the auditorium or an outdoor area.
- Reserve any needed equipment, such as a video-cassette recorder.

- Arrange for the custodian to help the Guest Readers transfer their equipment from their vehicle.
- If weapons will be brought onto campus, remember to get written permission from the principal.
- Decorate the bulletin board with a cut-out of a castle (or pictures of famous castles) and knights, lords, and ladies. Or decorate the bulletin board with characters from medieval folklore, such as Merlin, King Arthur and his Knights of the Round Table, or Robin Hood and his merry men.

INTRODUCTION OF THE GUEST READER

"Hear ye! Hear ye! Fair Ladies and Lords and all Worthy People! Greetings! I welcome thee with great happiness and am heartily pleased to introduce thee to today's Guest Readers (names) from (organization). They will verily bring the Middle Ages to life!"

Alternate Introduction

"When I went to school, my favorite subject was history. I loved to learn about people in the past—what they did and how they lived. Today, we are in for a treat. Not only will our Guests tell us about the age of lords, ladies, and knights, but they will make the Middle Ages come to life! Let's give a big welcome to (Guest Readers' names) from (organization)."

GUEST READER'S INTRODUCTION TO THE BOOK

"Knights were very important to society in the Middle Ages. You have heard of the great King Arthur and the Knights of the Round Table. This story is adapted from a fifteenth-century poem about one of Arthur's best-loved knights, Sir Gawain."

DISCUSSION TOPICS

Suggest to the Guest Reader to:

- Give a brief overview of the history of the Middle Ages:
    - the Middle Ages flourished from approximately the fifth century,

when the Roman Empire fell, to the end of the fifteenth century, when the Renaissance began

–the term "Middle Ages" (or *medieval,* which comes from the Latin word meaning the Middle Ages) was coined because the age is sandwiched between the classical period of Greek and Roman civilization and the Renaissance, when there was a rebirth in the arts and sciences and a turning away from the strictly religious view of life

–the early Middle Ages, from the fifth century to 1,000 A.D., is sometimes called the Dark Ages and refers mainly to what was going on in Europe at the time when ancient civilizations were under attack by many people, including Germanic tribes and nomadic tribes from eastern Asia. There was a great deal of fear, confusion, and social chaos. The constant threat of attacks led to the feudal system. (The Dark Ages also refers to the fact that because of the chaos, there are few surviving records from the period)

–"feudalism" is the term used to describe the social and economic structure of medieval society. Poor people became serfs, consenting to work for the lords on a manor in exchange for protection. And a nobleman, or a vassal, was given land by a lord in return for military assistance or other services to the lord

–because most of Europe lived under this system during the Middle Ages, the period is sometimes called the Age of Feudalism. It is also sometimes called the Age of Chivalry because of the code by which knights were supposed to conduct themselves on and off the battlefield

• Briefly explain feudal society, chivalry, and everyday life in a castle and village, including the role of women and children, marriage, education, religion, medicine, food, work, and leisure pastimes.

DEMONSTRATION

• Demonstrate crafts such as carding (a system of brushing wool between two boards fitted with wires to prepare it for spinning) and spinning wool into yarn (the fibers of wool were drawn from the top of the distaff with the fingers of one hand, while the other twisted and rotated the spindle).

- Play musical instruments and sing songs from the period.
- Describe clothing and armor. (Pass around a knight's helmet so the students can feel how heavy it is.)
- Engage in mock combat.

The Guest Readers who visited my school were representatives from the Society of Creative Anachronism. They took on the personas of characters from the Middle Ages, wearing period costumes and speaking in the vernacular of that time. They had an established presentation that involved the students as much as possible. (They even provided each student with a list of the Knight's Code.) The Society of Creative Anachronism truly did bring history to life!

KIDS' ACTIVITIES

Ask the students to:

- Learn terminology such as feudalism, villein, vassal, demesne, wattle and daub, motte-and-bailey, chivalry, haubert, quintain, oath of fealty, fief, trencher, solar, buttery, sumptuary laws, excommunication, heresy, barbarian, cutpurse. Create word puzzles and quiz games to test knowledge of vocabulary and information about the Middle Ages. The book, *How Would You Survive in the Middle Ages?* by Fiona Macdonald, provides a ready-made quiz that is fun to answer.
- Draw a timeline for the Early Middle Ages (Dark Ages), and another time-line for the Later Middle Ages. Books such as *The Roman Empire and the Dark Ages* by Giovanni Caselli, *The Middle Ages* by Sarah Howarth, *The Dark Ages* by Tony Gregory, *The Middle Ages* (Facts on File) by Fiona Macdonald, *The Middle Ages* (Silver Burdett) by Fiona Macdonald, *The Days of Knights & Castles* by Pierre Miquel, and *The Rise of Islam* by Anton Powell, will be helpful.
- Write a story, poem, or report about a famous person in the Middle Ages. Notable people include Attila the Hun, Rollo the Viking, Alfred the Great, William the Conqueror, Emperor Justinian, Empress Theodora, Eleanor of Aquitaine, Marco Polo, Genghis Khan, Joan of Arc, Johann Gutenberg, Muhammad, Pope Gregory, Saint Benedict, Saint Francis, Saint Clare, and

Abbess Hildegard of Bingen. Variation: In costume, give a presentation to the class from the perspective of a well-known person of the Middle Ages.

• Write a report about the Crusades. Describe how the Crusades impacted Western Europe in the Middle Ages, including the expansion of trade. In addition, explain how the Crusades impact our lives even today. For example, according to *The Crusades* by Ken Hills, the brutality displayed by both Christians and Moslems during the Crusades led to fear and suspicion between the two groups that has lasted to the present time. Many of the books listed in **RELATED BOOKS**, including historical fictions such as *The Road to Damietta* by Scott O'Dell and *The Ramsay Scallop* by Frances Temple, discuss the Crusades. Variation: Write a report about the Hundred Years War between England and France.

• The teacher breaks the class into groups, assigning each group with a specific aspect of medieval life to explore. Examples include the Crusades, the monastery, feudalism, town life and guilds, medicine, and the Black Death. Each group presents a general report that gives the rest of the class a brief understanding of the topic. Then each member of the group assumes a role of a person associated with the topic and tells his story to the class—thus providing additional details of what life was like in the Middle Ages. For instance, if the topic is the Crusades, the roles might include a Crusader Knight, a Saracen soldier, a pilgrim, Peter the Hermit, Saladin, a child crusader, a villager whose town was sacked, or a heretic.

• Present a "travelogue" on video or live that describes life in another part of the world during the Middle Ages such as Japan, China, India, Scandinavia, Russia, or the Americas. Books such as *The Medieval World* by Mike Corbishley, *The Middle Ages* by Mike Corbishley, *The Dark Ages* by Tony Gregory, and *The Samurai Castle* and *The Middle Ages* (Facts on File) by Fiona Macdonald, provide information. Variation: Create a travel brochure or travel-magazine article describing one of these lands and its culture. Include information on both the positive and negative aspects of its society. Alternatively, create a newspaper with articles that give readers an understanding of what life was like in that land.

- Pretend to be Marco Polo returning from thirteenth-century China. Describe the culture and land to the audience. Variation: Assume the role of a traveler returning from another culture. Give an eyewitness account of life in that other land. Use visual aids.

- Write a story describing the life of a Viking, a Frank, Goth, Lombard, Mongol, or another "barbaric" tribe. Read *The Roman Empire and the Dark Ages* by Giovanni Caselli, *The Early Middle Ages* by James A. Corrick, *The Early Middle Ages* by Monica Dambrosio and Roberto Barbieri, *The Dark Ages* by Tony Gregory, *The Middle Ages* (Facts on File) by Fiona Macdonald, the historical fiction *Hakon of Rogen's Saga* by Erik Christian Haugaard (about a young Viking), and other books for information.

- Write a report or create a poster comparing religions in the world during the medieval period, including Hinduism, Buddhism, Christianity, Islam, and Judaism. Several books, including *The Medieval World* by Mike Corbishley, *The Dark Ages* by Tony Gregory, *The Middle Ages* (Facts on File) by Fiona Macdonald, and *The Rise of Islam* by Anton Powell, cover this topic.

- Write a report or create a poster describing the different types of Christian beliefs, including Iconoclasm, Arianism, and the split between the Catholic and Orthodox churches. This subject is discussed in books, such as *The Early Middle Ages* by Monica Dambrosio and Roberto Barbieri and *The Dark Ages* by Tony Gregory.

- Recreate the badges Christian pilgrims wore to signify the shrines they visited. For example, a pilgrim who traveled to Jerusalem wore a badge with a palm leaf on it. Books such as *A Medieval Monk* by Giovanni Caselli, *Medieval People* by Sarah Howarth, *The Days of Knights & Castles* by Pierre Miquel, *Medieval Knights* by David Nicolle, and the historical fictions *The Road to Damietta* by Scott O'Dell and *The Ramsay Scallop* by Frances Temple provide information about pilgrims, religion, monks, and friars.

- Create a poster comparing the architecture (houses of worship, castles, cottages) found in Western Europe, Scandinavia, Moslem countries, Asian countries, and the Americas.

- Create a poster comparing and contrasting the Romanesque style of a cathedral and the Gothic style. Also discuss the Byzantine style of architecture. Books such as *The Middle Ages* by Mike Corbishley and *A Medieval Cathedral* by Fiona Macdonald will be helpful.

- Because most people in the Middle Ages could not read or understand the Latin words in religious services, the Church taught Christianity with statues and pictures of Bible stories and scenes from the Saints' lives painted on the walls and depicted in stained-glass windows. Five windows in the Cathedral of Augsburg, Germany are thought to be the oldest existing stained-glass windows, dating from the end of the 1000's and early 1100's. Each window shows a Biblical prophet. Before the 1100's, stained-glass windows were small. The Church of St. Denis, near Paris, was the first church to be built in the Gothic style and the first to have large stained-glass windows. The earliest windows date from the mid-1100's.

  Design a stained-glass window. For instructions, check out *Knights* by Rachel Wright. To find more information about stained-glass windows, read books such as *Medieval Life* by Andrew Langley, *A Medieval Cathedral* by Fiona Macdonald, and the historical fiction, *Proud Taste for Scarlet and Miniver* by E. L. Konigsburg.

- Create a poster showing how castles improved over the years.

- Write a report describing the rooms in a castle. In addition, build a model of a castle. Find directions in *Make Your Own Model: Forts & Castles* by Richard Cummings, illustrated by the author (New York: David McKay, 1977); *The Knight' Handbook* by Christopher Gravett; *Build Your Own Castle* by Kate Petty, illustrated by Louise Nevett (New York: Franklin Watts, 1985); *Castles* by Rachel Wright, and *Knights* by Rachel Wright. Variation: Write a report describing cathedrals and build a model.

- Create a castle that can be used as a letter-holder or a bank by gluing paper towel tubes to each corner of a square tissue box. Paint the castle and glue on paper windows and gate. For directions, read *The Best Holiday Crafts Ever!* by Kathy Ross, art by Sharon Lane Holm (Brookfield, CT: Millbrook, 1997).

- Create a mobile or booklet (in the shape of a castle) that provides unusual facts about castles. Here are a few examples:

–in 1066, when William the Conqueror won the Battle of Hastings, he had a motte-and-bailey castle constructed in one day because he brought pre-cut timbers on his ships. It was a prefabricated castle!

–in castles, the spiral stairs turned up and around to the right so that an attacker's sword arm would be hampered by the wall. He would have little space to use his arm at full range

–kings controlled potentially rebellious nobles by keeping control of castles. No one could build a castle without permission from the king. If a noble was suspected of disloyalty or if he built a castle illegally, the king would have the castle pulled down

This information was culled from the books listed in **RELATED BOOKS**.

- Write an "eyewitness" news report of a siege of a castle. Include a description of the type of castle, such as a motte-and-bailey; the tactics of the siege, such as starving the enemy or using sappers to undermine the castle walls; the defense strategy, such as "Greek fire"; and the siege weapons such as a trebuchet, a mangonel, or a ballista. Be sure the descriptions are true to the period.

- Write a report about one famous castle. Include pictures of the castle or create a model of it. Books such as *Castles of the Middle Ages* by Philippe Brochard and *The Truth About Castles* by Gillian Clements provide information.

- A few famous castles are said to be haunted. *Castles,* by Beth Smith, recounts ghost stories associated with these castles. Write a haunted-castle story. (It does not have to be about a real castle.)

- Set up a Middle Ages exhibit that children from other classes can visit. Each booth or station in the exhibit demonstrates a specific aspect of the Middle Ages. For example, at the Black Death station, "victims" made up to look as if they have sores (or buboes), quietly moan and act ill. A student dressed as a monk gives a brief talk about the plague to the audience. At another station, students dressed as a squire and a knight describe a suit of armor, the education of a knight, the dubbing ceremony, tournaments, and chivalry. All the demonstrations should be the same amount of time, no longer than 3–5 minutes. (The exact time should be determined in advance.) The demonstrations are given simultaneously.

The audience is divided into small groups. Each group is assigned to a specific station. At the end of the 3 minutes (or longer), the leader of the exhibit (the teacher) rings a bell to signal the groups to rotate to the next station and demonstration.

• Produce a medieval fair with booths that sell jewelry, headwear, ribbons, garlands, leather goods, medicinal herbs, candles, foods (chews—meat pies, fritters, gingerbread, "ale"), etc. Include dancing, such as dancing around the maypole, and games, such as archery (use arrows with rubber suction-cup tips). In addition, have puppet shows, minstrels, mummers, jugglers, and trained "animals" (students in costume) for entertainment. Many of the books listed in **RELATED BOOKS** describe fairs and festivals, including *The Middle Ages* by Giovanni Caselli, *Medieval Life* by Andrew Langley, and *A Medieval Castle* by Fiona Macdonald. Fairs also figure in the storylines of much of the historical fiction, including *Catherine, Called Birdy* and *The Midwife's Apprentice,* both by Karen Cushman, *The Door in the Wall* by Marguerite de Angeli, *Adam of the Road* by Elizabeth Janet Gray, *The Road to Damietta* by Scott O'Dell, and *Jackaroo* by Cynthia Voight. Variation: Create a marketplace with booths where shopkeepers, such as an apothecary, sell their wares. A poster and/or report describing the shopkeeper's job, the way his/her shop looks, and his/her everyday life in the village are/is displayed at each booth. Students barter for goods at each booth. Good descriptions of shops in town can be found in *The Roman Empire and the Dark Ages* by Giovanni Caselli, *Medieval Places* by Sarah Howarth, and *A Medieval City* by R. J. Unstead.

• Medieval theatre was introduced by the Church, at first in the form of simple pantomimes of the Nativity at Christmas or the Resurrection at Easter. Then short dramatic scenes became part of special festival services performed in the church by the clergy. A scene depicted a great episode in the Bible such as Noah and the flood. The scenes proved to be so popular that they were moved outside to the church porch. The dramas evolved into one-act plays spoken in Latin and eventually translated into the vernacular. By the thirteenth century they had become a complete cycle of plays depicting the sacred history of the Christian world and could last as long as 40 days. In the later Middle Ages these religious plays, also known as "passion" or mystery plays, were staged by the local guilds. Each guild chose a story associated with their craft. For example, the carpenters portrayed the building of Noah's ark. The dramas were now performed at stations or on wagons in the marketplace where more people could see them. Added to the repertory of medieval drama were the saint plays or "miracle" plays, and the morality plays with allegorical characters such as Good Deed and Death. Eventually, social commentary, even criticism of the Church, entered into the plays. This provoked religious authorities to try to ban them but the plays were too popular to stop. Although women could be members of the audience, only men were allowed to perform in plays. It was considered immoral for women to act. The play *Everyman*, from the fifteenth century, is the best known from the medieval period; it deals with the crisis of facing death.

Read or perform plays from the Middle Ages. Plays and information about medieval drama can be found in *A Treasury of the Theatre: From Aeschylus To Ostrovsky*, edited by John Gassner (New York: Simon & Schuster, 1967). Excerpts from plays are printed in *Medieval Holidays and Festivals*, by Madeleine Pelner Cosman. Variation: Write an original passion play and present it to the class.

For additional information about medieval drama, read books such as *Living in Castle Times* by Robyn Gee, *Medieval Life* by Andrew Langley, *A Medieval Cathedral* by Fiona Macdonald, and *A Medieval City* by R. J. Unstead. Medieval theatre drives the plot in *A Little Lower Than the Angels* by Geraldine McCaughrean, but also is involved in *Catherine, Called Birdy* by Karen Cushman, *Adam of the Road* by Elizabeth Janet Gray, *The Ramsay Scallop* by Frances Temple, and *Jackaroo* by Cynthia Voight.

- Recreate a medieval wedding and feast (or only a medieval feast). Refer to listed books, including *A Medieval Feast* by Aliki, *Medieval Holidays and Festivals* by Madeleine Pelner Cosman, *The Knight's Handbook* by Christopher Gravett, and *Merry Ever After* by Joe Lasker, for information. Many of the fictional books, including *Catherine, Called Birdy* by Karen Cushman, *Men of Iron* by Howard Pyle, *The Lady of Rhuddesmere* by Victoria Strauss, and *Jackaroo* by Cynthia Voight describe weddings and/or feasts.

How Would You Survive in the Middle Ages? by Fiona Macdonald and Cosman's and Gravett's books provide menus and recipes for meals eaten during the medieval era. (Cosman's *Medieval Holidays and Festivals* is especially helpful.)

- In the medieval era people primarily ate with their fingers. According to *The Days of Knights & Castles* by Pierre Miquel, when Piers Gaveston, a friend of King Edward II (1307–1327), tried to introduce the use of forks at meals, most English people thought it was a horrible foreign custom. Many of the ideas of courtly love, manners, and chivalry were developed in Eleanor of Aquitaine's court. Some of these rules, such as opening a door for a woman, are still observed today.

Write a report or create a poster comparing medieval manners to modern ones. Variation: Assume the role of an etiquette expert living in the Middle Ages. Write a pamphlet describing proper etiquette, write a "Dear Emily Post" or "Dear Miss Manners" advice type of newspaper column, or deliver a "lecture" on proper etiquette to the young "nobility" in class. Books such as the Miquel book, *Castles of the Middle Ages* by Philippe Brochard, *The Knight's Handbook* by Christopher Gravett, *A Medieval Castle* and *The Middle Ages* (Silver Burdett) by Fiona Macdonald, *Medieval Knights* by David Nicolle, *Castles* by Philip Steele, and historical fiction such as *Max and Me and the Time Machine* by Gery Greer and Bob Ruddick, discuss this topic. The novel *Proud Taste for Scarlet and Miniver,* by E. L. Konigsburg, describes the development of courtly love and manners.

- Produce a sports newscast for a joust or tournament. The Herald is the "sports announcer." *Harold the Herald* by Dana Fradon gives a complete picture of the Herald's duties. In addition, check out *The Knight's Handbook* by Christopher Gravett and *Knights* by Rachel Wright for instructions on creating a miniature joust.

- Play games that were popular in the medieval era such as chess, backgammon, and blind-man's bluff. For information regarding leisure activities, read books, including *Board and Table Games From Many Civilizations* by R. C. Bell, illustrated by Rosalind H. Leadley, photographs by Kenneth Watson (London: Oxford University Press, 1960); *Medieval Holidays and Festivals* by Madeleine Pelner Cosman; *The Knight's Handbook* by Christopher Gravett;

The Middle Ages by Sarah Howarth; and *How Would You Survive in the Middle Ages?* by Fiona Macdonald.

- Produce a commercial promoting medieval-era games and toys (chess, dice, spinning tops, rolling hoops, etc.) and sports (falconry, archery, etc.). Variation: Create a commercial promoting a fair, festival, or tournament, or produce a commercial selling a castle, armor, or medicinal herbs.

- Design a coat-of-arms and a pennant. In addition to Fradon's *Harold the Herald*, many of the books listed in the bibliography explain heraldry, including *Castles of the Middle Ages* by Philippe Brochard, *Illuminations* by Jonathan Hunt, *Medieval People* by Sarah Howarth, *The Middle Ages* (Silver Burdett) by Fiona Macdonald, *Medieval Knights* by David Nicolle, and *The Days of Knights & Castles* by Pierre Miquel. *The Knight's Handbook* by Christopher Gravett provides directions on how to make a shield of arms, and *Knights* by Rachel Wright gives instructions on how to create a coat-of-arms stained-glass window. Variation: Using fabric pens, draw the coat-of-arms on a white T-shirt. Remember to put a paper bag between the front and back of the shirt because the pens might bleed through. Another idea is to make a place mat by drawing the coat-of-arms on a white paper mat. Cover it with clear contact paper.

- Create a poster or write a report tracing the development of armor from hauberks (coats of mail) in the eleventh and twelfth centuries to the late fifteenth century when plate armor was perfected and knights were completely covered. For information, refer to the books listed **RELATED BOOKS**, including *Knights in Armor* by John D. Clare, *Knights in Shining Armor* by Gail Gibbons, *Knight* by Christopher Gravett, *Medieval Knights* by David Nicolle, and *The Medieval Knight* by Martin Windrow.

- Have a costume parade that visits classrooms in the school. Each costumed student portrays a different medieval character such as a monk, serf, noble, minstrel, or knight. At designated classrooms a presentation can be given where each character briefly explains his role in medieval life and talks about his clothes. The presentation should also include a description of the sumptuary laws, where poor people were forbidden to wear the kind of clothing usually worn by nobility. Books such as *The Middle Ages* by Sarah

Howarth, *Medieval Life* by Andrew Langley, *The Days of Knights & Castles* by Pierre Miquel, and *Kings, Queens, Knights & Jesters: Making Medieval Costumes* by Lynn Edelman Schnurberger, will be helpful.

- Create the types of masks mummers would wear.

- Pretend an ancestor's trunk has been discovered in the attic. Inside are artifacts from the Middle Ages such as a sword and shield, a purse, a ring, a shepherd's horn-pipe. Give a presentation to the class explaining these artifacts and how they related to the ancestor's life.

- Books such as *The Dark Ages* by Tony Gregory and *How Would You Survive in the Middle Ages?* by Fiona Macdonald, explain how some of the information about the medieval era was developed from items found at archaeological excavations. Medieval trash such as broken pieces of pottery or jewelry gives clues as to how people lived during that period. Rumage through the family trash and write an essay from the point of view of a future archaeologist, theorizing the way in which people in our period lived.

- Historians also learn about the Middle Ages and how the people lived through documents. The Domesday Book, made for King William I in 1086, was a record of who owned land in England and how the land was farmed and used. Soon after Edward I was crowned in 1274, a detailed survey of his realm, called the Hundred Rolls of 1275, was done. The king's representatives traveled throughout the land with questionnaires that recorded the people's comments and complaints.

  Create a school Domesday Book/Hundred Rolls. Ask the students about their personal property; their likes and dislikes in music, films, books, television shows; their opinions and feelings about school, their home life, and current events throughout the world; and how they think society treats kids. The survey should give an indication of how young people in the community live and what they think are important issues. Books such as Sheila Sancha's *Walter Dragun's Town* provide additional information about the Domesday Book and the Hundred Rolls of 1275.

- Art also provides clues as to how people lived in the Middle Ages. For example, in *Castles of the Middle Ages*, Brochard writes about the Book of Hours, a small prayer book with illustrations depicting medieval people going about their daily activities. *The Luttrell Village* by Sheila Sancha describes the Luttrell Psalter, a prayer book made for Sir George Luttrell and illustrated with drawings of Luttrell, his family, and the people in his village as they went about their work.

Draw a self-portrait or a picture of a family member, friend, or neighbor involved in an everyday activity. Then draw a picture of the same person, as if s/he lived in the Middle Ages, performing the same type of task. For example, a present-day mother cooking at the stove translates into a medieval era mother cooking over an open pit. Another example: a friend playing the electric guitar becomes a minstrel playing a lute.

• The Bayeux Tapestry is not actually a tapestry because it is not woven. It is an embroidery made to commemorate the Norman victory at the Battle of Hastings in 1066. The picture and words on the embroidery record the events that led to William the Conqueror's successful invasion. The work was probably completed in England within 10 years of the famous battle; it was then taken to be displayed in Bayeux, France.

Create a "tapestry" that records an important event in the Middle Ages, an important current event, or an important personal event. Draw pictures and write captions on a long piece of butcher-block paper. Variation: Draw the pictures with fabric pens on a long piece of cloth material. Remember to put a paper bag under the fabric because the pens can bleed through. Use embroidery yarn to stitch an outline of the pictures. For instructions to make a fabric frieze, check out *Knights* by Rachel Wright. To make a tapestry, find directions in Wright's book, *Castles*.

Many arts-and-craft projects and activities related to the Middle Ages are provide in Wright's books and in *The Knight's Handbook* by Christopher Gravett, *Build Your Own Castle* by Kate Petty, illustrated by Louise Nevett (New York: Franklin Watts, 1985), and *Merlin's Magic: A Reading Activities Idea Book for Use with Children,* edited by Carol H. Thomas, illustrated by Paul D. Gaudette (Phoenix, AZ: Oryx, 1984). For information about the Bayeux Tapestry, refer to resource materials such as *The Medieval World* and *The Middle Ages* by Mike Corbishley, *Knight* by

Christopher Gravett, *The Middle Ages* by Sarah Howarth, and *The Middle Ages* (Facts on File) by Fiona Macdonald.

- Sewing and embroidery were two important activities in the medieval era. Learn to sew or embroider by using sewing cards and embroidery kits.

- Sheila Sancha provides maps of the villages in *The Luttrell Village* and *Walter Dragun's Town.* Draw maps of students' own neighborhoods.

- A chronicler wrote down the history of events—the news of the day. Assume the role of a medieval chronicler and describe an event. Then become a modern-day chronicler and report a current event. Variation: Write a chronicle of a current event but translate it into Middle-Ages terms. For example, describe a professional baseball game as a new kind of tournament. Another example: Explain the AIDS virus as yet another plague. Remember to use the vernacular of the period. Read *Medieval People* by Sarah Howarth for a good description of a chronicler.

- Write a report comparing education in the Middle Ages to today's system in the United States. *Medieval Places* by Sarah Howarth, *The Middle Ages* by Sarah Howarth, *The Middle Ages* (Silver Burdett) by Fiona Macdonald, and *The Days of Knights & Castles* by Pierre Miquel are a few of the books listed in the bibliography that discuss this topic. Variation: Write a description of a typical day in school, then write a description of a typical day in school from the perspective of a student in the Middle Ages.

- Learn about the legal system in medieval Europe. Then recreate a court scene to demonstrate how the law operated in that era. Books such as *Medieval Places* by Sarah Howarth, *Life in a Medieval Village* by Gwyneth Morgan, and historical fiction such as *Proud Taste for Scarlet and Miniver* by E. L. Konigsburg, provide information.

- Create a poster that traces the seeds of democracy. Include information about Henry II (1133–1189), who laid the foundation of the court system in England; the Magna Carta signed by King John of England in 1215; and the beginnings of modern parliamentary government that appeared under Edward I of England (1272–1307) and also began to develop in France under King Philip IV (1285–1314).

- Many of the books in **RELATED BOOKS**, including *Anno's Medieval World* and *The Black Death* by James Day, and the historical fictions, *The Midwife's Apprentice* by Karen Cushman, *The Trumpeter of Krakow* by Eric P. Kelly, *A Little Lower Than the Angels* by Geraldine McCaughrean, *What Happened in Hamelin* by Gloria Skurzynski, *The Lady of Rhuddesmere* by Victoria Strauss, and *The Ramsay Scallop* by Frances Temple, discuss the limited knowledge people had in medieval Europe—especially in the areas of medicine and science. Superstition figured prominently in the thinking of the time. Discuss some of these ideas. Include information about the study of alchemy and astrology. Although these ideas may seem outlandish to us, there are people in the modern world who hold onto superstitions or have "nonscientific" explanations of the world's phenomena. Give examples and discuss these ideas as well. In addition, many of the listed books describe medieval society's intolerance of others with differing beliefs. Have people changed very much since the Middle Ages? Write an essay or discuss with classmates this topic.

- *Anno's Medieval World* talks about the theories in astronomy that were developed during the Middle Ages. Study these ideas. Then check news sources to find the most recent information regarding space exploration and astronomy. In addition, look through a telescope to study the planets and stars and read books on astronomy such as *The Night Sky Book: An Everyday Guide to Every Night* by Jamie Jobb, illustrated by Linda Bennett (Boston: Little, Brown, 1977).

- Create a poster that lists inventions and explorations that occurred during the Middle Ages. Books such as *The Middle Ages* (Silver Burdett) by Fiona Macdonald will be helpful. The Caselli books, *The Roman Empire and the Dark Ages* and *The Middle Ages*, have excellent descriptions of the technological developments during this period.

- Merlin is the renown wizard/magician of Arthurian legends. Become a magician too! Learn magic tricks from books geared to young people such as *Magic Fun,* edited by Marilyn Baillie, photographs by Ray Boudreau, illustrated by Josephine Cheng and Vesna Krstanovich (Boston: Little, Brown, 1992). Astound friends with tricks based on scientific principles. For ideas, read books such as *Magic Tricks, Science Facts* by Friedhoffer, The Madman of Magic, photographs by Timothy White, illustrated by Richard Kaufman (New York: Franklin Watts, 1990) and *175 Experiments to Amuse and Amaze Your Friends: Experiments! Tricks! Things to Make!* by Brenda Walpole, illustrated by Kuo Kang Chen and Peter Bull (New York: Random House, 1988). Also, learn math tricks by reading books such as *Mathemagic* by Raymond Blum, illustrated by Jeff Sinclair (New York: Sterling, 1991).

- Cast "spells"—turning fellow classmates into monkeys, dogs, rabbits, giants, etc. Each child gets a chance to be Merlin. The child playing Merlin wears a Wizard's hat and waves a magic wand while chanting a few magic words and then saying, "I turn you into a _____!" The other children act out the animal or character named in the spell. After one or two spells, another child gets a turn to be Merlin. Variation: Organize a race. The children line up at a starting point. Merlin says, "I turn you into a _____!" The other children must travel to the finish line, moving like the character or animal named in the spell. For example, if Merlin turns the players into rabbits, they must hop to the finish line.

- Write and present a skit based on a medieval legend or folk tale such as Robin Hood or King Arthur. Variation: Create skits that depict a historical event such as an episode from the Crusades or of every-day life in the Middle Ages.

- There are many versions of folk tales; for example, *Sir Gawain and the Loathly Damsel* by Joanna Troughton, *Sir Gawain and the Loathly Lady* by Selina Hastings, and "Gawain and the Loathely Lady" in *The Sword and the Circle* by Rosemary Sutcliff. ("The Wife of Bath's Tale" in Chaucer's *The Canterbury Tales* is a different spin of the basic plot.) Choose a well-known legend and retell it in the form of a story, poem, or song. Variation: Write an original legend.

- Write a story (historical fiction) that takes place in the Middle Ages. Decorate the pages with illuminations.

- Write a story from the perspective of a modern-day person who travels back in time to the Middle Ages. Read about time-travelers in *Max and Me and the Time Machine* by Gery Greer and Bob Ruddick, *The Time Trekkers Visit the Middle Ages* by Kate Needham, and *The Knight at Dawn* by Mary Pope Osborne.

- *Catherine, Called Birdy* by Karen Cushman is a diary of a young girl describing her life in her father's castle. Choose a role of a person in the Middle Ages, such as a serf, the head of a guild, an apprentice, a journeyman, a minstrel, a priest, a nun, etc. Write a diary from the perspective of that person. Include information about the person's family, housing, clothing, job, how s/he got the job, primary concerns, leisure activities, religion, government, illnesses, etc. (*Hint:* The teacher should assign the students their roles by writing different characters on separate slips of paper. The students pick the slips out of a bag. Otherwise, if students are allowed to choose their own roles, they may all write about knights!)

- In the book *The Ramsay Scallop* by Frances Temple, the character Etienne comments on how Bible stories and folk tales can be used to shape people's attitudes, such as society's view of the woman's role in the world. Give examples of this in the Middle Ages, and then give examples of how current attitudes are shaped by television shows, films, and music.

- The issues of infatuation with a charismatic person and mob mentality are explored in several books, including *The Trumpeter of Krakow* by Eric P. Kelly, *A Little Lower Than the Angels* by Geraldine McCaughrean, *The Road to Damietta* by Scott O'Dell, *What Happened in Hamelin* by Gloria Skurzynski, and *The Lady of Rhuddesmere* by Victoria Strauss. Describe real-life examples that have occurred throughout the ages.

- Read one of the novels listed in **RELATED BOOKS**. Fix the time-period for when the story takes place. Write a report summarizing the historical events during that period. Do these events impact the story?

- Participate in an Age of Chivalry obstacle course. Here are a few ideas for stations:

  –Station 1: *Pin the Tail on the Dragon*

  This is a variation of the party game, "Pin the Tail on the Donkey." A picture of a dragon, sans tail, is drawn on a poster. The poster is attached to a wall. Give the player a dragon's tail made out of poster board. (Be sure to place double stick tape on the back of the tail.) Place a blindfold over the player's eyes. Turn him 3 times and point him in the direction of the poster.

Unaided, the player walks the few feet to the poster and tapes the tail onto the picture of the dragon. Because the player is blindfolded, the tail will probably be attached anywhere but where a tail should be!

–Station 2: *Escape Tunnel*

Decorate a large packing box to look like a castle. Cut out an arch in the front and back of the box, thus creating a tunnel. The player crawls through the tunnel.

–Station 3: *The Queen's Favor*

Hang a chiffon or silk scarf from a tree or from a tall structure. The player must jump to tap the Queen's scarf. (Do not hang the scarf too high.)

–Station 4: *Moat Crossing*

A wide strip of butcher-block paper represents the moat; or a rope held a few inches off the ground by two assistants can represent the moat. The player must jump over the moat.

–Station 5: *Coat of Arms Toss*

Decorate a bean bag with a coat of arms. The player must toss the bean bag into a box decorated to look like a castle. Variation: Toss ghosts into a haunted castle. To create a ghost, place a white cloth over a tennis ball. Gather the cloth under the ball and tie it with black yarn. Draw two eyes with a black marker.

–Station 6: *Fun at the Fair*

The player must juggle two sponge balls (or three chiffon scarfs). The balls must change hands three times.

–Station 7: *Bowling for Damsels*

Decorate one-quart milk cartons to look like castles. Set them up in bowling-pin formation. The player tries to knock down the pins using a rubber playground ball.

–Station 8: *"X" Marks the Spot*

A picture of an evil knight is taped to a wall. The player "suits up." (He places a helmet on his head, picks up a cardboard shield and cardboard sword.) The player must make the motion of an "X" on the evil knight's body with the sword. (*The Knight's Handbook* by Christopher Gravett, and *Knights* by Rachel Wright provide instructions on how to make the props.)

The individual or team that goes through the obstacle course with the best time is dubbed "knight" and given a pennant as prize. If the obstacle course is not planned as a competition, do not time the players and dub as knight everyone who participates. (*Hint:* To keep the game moving at a lively pace and to avoid children from waiting too long for their turn, have each player begin the course when the child in front of him begins the third station. This should only be done if the activity is not planned as a competition.)

Videos

Instructional Video

- *Castle* (Unicorn Projects, 1983. Live action and animated. 55 minutes)

  During part of the video, David Macaulay, author and illustrator of *Castle* (see **Related Books**), leads a tour of a standing, ancient Welsh castle.

Films on Video

Films Retelling Historic Events

- *Becket,* starring Richard Burton and Peter O'Toole (E&M Enterprising, 1964/MPI Home Video, 1989. 150 minutes. Not rated)

  Beckett is the closest confidant to King Henry II, but when the King appoints him Archbishop of Canterbury, Beckett's allegiance changes. He becomes devoted to God and comes into conflict with the King. This leads to tragedy. The film is based on the Jean Anouilh play.

- *Joan of Arc,* starring Ingrid Bergman, Jose Ferrer, and Ward Bond (Distributed by Image Entertainment. 100 minutes. Not rated)

  This 1948 film portrays the story of the girl who, inspired by God, leads the French against the British invaders, only to be captured by the enemy. She is tried for blasphemy and burned at the stake. The movie is based on the play, *Joan of Lorraine,* by Maxwell Anderson.

- *The Lion in Winter,* starring Peter O'Toole and Katharine Hepburn (Embassy Pictures 1967 /Embassy Home Entertainment, 1986. 134 minutes. Rated PG)

Based on the play by James Goldman, the film depicts the conflict between King Henry II and Queen Eleanor of Aquitaine as she plots and connives to insure her eldest son's position as heir to the throne, while the King, favoring his youngest son for the title, counterattacks.

Films Retelling the Robin Hood Legend

- *The Adventures of Robin Hood,* starring Errol Flynn, Olivia de Havilland, Basil Rathbone, and Claude Rains (Warner Brothers, 1938/ MGM/UA Home Video. 103 minutes. Not rated)

- *Robin Hood* (Walt Disney Pictures 1973/Walt Disney Home Video. Animated. 83 minutes. Rated G)

  This musical version of Robin Hood is told with animal characters.

- *The Story of Robin Hood and His Merrie Men,* starring Richard Todd, Joan Rice, and Peter Finch (Walt Disney, 1952/Walt Disney Home Video. 84 minutes. Not rated)

Films Retelling the King Arthur Legend

- *Camelot,* starring Richard Harris, Vanessa Redgrave, Franco Nero, David Hemmings, and Lionel Jeffries (Warner Brothers, 1967/Warner Home Video. 178 minutes. Rated G)

  Based on the Broadway musical by Alan Jay Lerner and Frederick Loewe, the film recounts the story of the idealized Kingdom destroyed by the passion between King Arthur's Guinevere and the Knight, Sir Lancelot.

- *The Sword and the Stone* (Walt Disney, 1963/Walt Disney Home Video. Animated. 79 minutes. Rated G)

  Based on the book by T. H. White, the film depicts the time when the boy Arthur pulls the sword, Excalibur, from the stone.

Films Based on Mark Twain's Book, *A Connecticut Yankee in King Arthur's Court*

- *A Connecticut Yankee in King Arthur's Court*, starring Bing Crosby, Rhonda Fleming, William Bendix, and Sir Cedric Hardwicke (Paramount Pictures, 1949/MCA Home Video, 1987. 108 minutes. Not rated)

  This is a musical version about the turn-of-the-century New Englander who is knocked unconscious and finds himself awake in sixth-century Camelot. The score is by Jimmy Van Heusen and Johnny Burke.

- *A Connecticut Yankee in King Arthur's Court*, starring Keshia Knight Pulliam, Michael Gross, and Jean Marsh (A Schaefer/Karpf Production/Family Home Entertainment, 1989. 95 minutes. Not rated)

  A Connecticut schoolgirl bumps her head and wakes up in King Arthur's court.

- *A Kid in King Arthur's Court*, starring Thomas Ian Nicholas, Joss Ackland, and Art Malik (Walt Disney Pictures, n.d. 90 minutes. Rated PG)

  An earthquake sends a 14-year-old Little Leaguer back in time to King Arthur's court.

Films Retelling the Sir Walter Scott Classic, *Ivanhoe*

This is the story about a young Saxon knight who returns to twelfth-century England after fighting with Richard the Lion-Hearted in the Crusades, only to find that his love, Rowena, has been betrothed to another and Richard's throne has been usurped by his evil brother, Prince John. Ivanhoe must fight to save Rowena, to restore Richard to the throne, and to protect Rebecca of York.

- *Ivanhoe*, starring Robert Taylor, Elizabeth Taylor, and Joan Fontaine (MGM Presents, 1952/ MGM /UA HOME Video/Turner. 107 minutes. Not rated)

- *Ivanhoe*, starring James Mason, Anthony Andrews, Olivia Hussey, and Lysette Anthony (Rosemont Productions in association with Columbia Pictures Television, 1982/RCA–Columbia Pictures Home Video. 142 minutes. Not rated)

This was a made-for-TV movie.

• *Ivanhoe* (Children's Video of America/Troll Associates, 1988. Animated. 50 minutes. Not rated)

Film Based on the Book by Kenneth Grahame

• *The Reluctant Dragon* (Walt Disney/Walt Disney Home Video, 1987. Animated. 28 minutes. Not rated)

SONGS

Show/Movie Tunes

• *Camelot* (Vocal Selections), words by Alan Jay Lerner and music by Frederick Loewe. New York: Charles Hansen Music and Books/ n.p.: Chappell, 1960.

• *Pippin* (Vocal Selections), words and music by Stephen Schwartz. n.p.: Jobete Music/Bewin-Mills Publishing, 1972.

This Broadway musical is about Charlemagne's son.

• from *The Reluctant Dragon* (animated Disney film based on the book):

  –"The Reluctant Dragon," words by Ed Penner and music by Charles Wolcott, p. 30 in *Disney Fake Book*. New York: Bourne/ Milwaukee, WI: Hal Leonard, 1996.

• from *Robin Hood* (animated Disney film, 1973):

  –"Love," words by Floyd Huddleston and music by George Bruns, p. 99 in *Disney Fake Book*.

  –"Oo-De-Lally," words and music by Roger Miller, p. 115 in *Disney Fake Book*. (This can also be found in *The Illustrated Treasury of Disney Songs* [New York: Hyperion/Milwaukee, WI: Hal Leonard, 1993], p. 128.)

• from *The Sword in the Stone* (animated Disney film, 1963):

  –"Blue Oak Tree," words and music by Richard M. Sherman and Robert B. Sherman, p. 21 in *Disney Fake Book*.

  –"Higitus Figitus (Merlin's Magic Song)," words and music by Richard M. Sherman and Robert B. Sherman, p. 68 in *Disney*

Fake Book. (This can also be found in *The Illustrated Treasury of Disney Songs,* p. 93.)

–"A Most Befuddling Thing," words and music by Richard M. Sherman and Robert B. Sherman, p. 110 in *Disney Fake Book.*

–"That's What Makes the World Go 'Round," words and music by Richard M. Sherman and Robert B. Sherman, p. 160 in *Disney Fake Book.*

Most of these songs have been recorded.

Songs Written During the Middle Ages or That Include References to the Middle Ages

• "The Battle of Harlaw" (describing an encounter that took place in 1411), p. 39 in *Songs of England, Ireland & Scotland: A Bonnie Bunch of Roses* by Dan Milner. New York: Oak Publications, 1983.

• "Bold Robin Hood" (this version is by Mrs. Cal Hicks), p. 124 in *American Folk Tales and Songs: And Other Examples of English–American Tradition as Preserved in the Appalachian Mountains and Elsewhere in the United States,* by Richard Chase, illustrated by Joshua Tolford. New York: Dover, 1971.

• "The Cutty Wren," p. 12 in *Songs of the British Isles,* by Jerry Silverman. Pacific, MO: Mel Bay, 1993.

• "Good King Arthur," p. 28 in *How Many Strawberries Grow in the Sea?,* by Earl Bichel, illustrated by George Suyeoka. Chicago: Follett, 1969.

• "Lord Bateman" (probably about Gilbert à Becket, Saint Thomas's father), p. 24 in *Songs of England,* by Jerry Silverman. Pacific, MO: Mel Bay, 1991.

  This can also be found in *Songs of England, Ireland & Scotland: A Bonnie Bunch of Roses,* p. 25.

• *One Hundred English Folksongs,* edited by Cecil J. Sharp. New York: Dover, 1975. Includes many songs, such as "Bruton Town" (p. 4), "The Knight and the Shepherd's Daughter" (p. 6), and "Robin Hood and the Tanner" (p. 8).

• "Robin Hood and Little John," p. 37 in *Songs of England, Ireland & Scotland: A Bonnie Bunch of Roses.*

- "Thomas the Rhymer," p. 21 in *Songs of England, Ireland & Scotland: A Bonnie Bunch of Roses.*

Books That Include Songs From the Middle Ages and Information About Medieval Music

- *Historical Anthology of Music by Women,* edited by James R. Briscoe. Bloomington: Indiana University Press, 1987.

- *Medieval Music,* by John Caldwell. Bloomington: Indiana University Press, 1978.

- *Performing Medieval and Renaissance Music: An Introductory Guide,* by Elizabeth V. Phillips and John-Paul Christopher Jackson. New York: Schirmer, 1986.

- *Women in Music: An Anthology of Source Readings from the Middle Ages to the Present,* edited by Carol Neuls-Bates. New York: Harper & Row, 1982.

  Lyrics only.

Recordings of Medieval Music: A Small Sample of Recordings That Are Available

- *The Medieval Experience.* Archiv Produktion (449 082 2).

- *Music of the Crusades* (The Early Music Consort of London–David Munrow). London Records (430 264-2).

- *Now Make We Merthe: Medieval English Lyrics, Rounds and Carols.* Boston Skyline (B S D 121).

- *Trouveres—Courtly Love Songs From Northern France* and *Sequentia.* BMG Classics (77155-2-RC).

Recordings of Gregorian Chants

- *Chant* (The Benedictine Monks of Santo Domingo De Silos). Angel Records (CDC 7243 5 55138 2 3).

- *Chant II* (The Benedictine Monks of Santo Domingo De Silos). Angel Records (CDC 7243 5 55504 2 2).

- *Chant III* (The Benedictine Monks of Santo Domingo De Silos). Angel Records (7243 5 56202 2 4).

- *A Treasury of Gregorian Chants.* Independent/Distributed by Distributions (CLJ-2-5612).

MAGAZINES

The following publications are about history in general. There are publications about the medieval era, but they are of a scholarly nature and are geared towards adults:

- *Calliope*
  7 School Street
  Peterborough, NH 03458-1454
  (603) 924-7209

- *Children's Historical Newsletter*
  11 E. Main Street
  P.O. Box 505
  Mooresville, IN 46158
  (317) 831-1044

POETRY

- "The Battle of Agincourt," by Michael Drayton, p. 172 in *A New Treasury of Poetry,* compiled by Neil Philip, illustrated by John Lawrence. New York: Stewart, Tabori & Chang, 1990.

- "The Douglas Tragedy" (traditional), p. 190 in *A New Treasury of Poetry.*

- "Eldorado," by Edgar Allan Poe, p. 207 in *A New Treasury of Poetry.*

- "The Good Joan," by Lizette Woodworth Reese, p. 23 in *The Arbuthnot Anthology of Children's Literature* (4th ed., rev.), selected by May Hill Arbuthnot, Dorothy M. Broderick, Shelton L. Root, Jr., Mark Taylor, and Evelyn L. Wenzel, illustrated by various artists. New York: Lothrop, Lee & Shepard, 1976.

- "King Arthur" (traditional), p. 210 in *A New Treasury of Poetry.* (See "Good King Arthur" in **SONGS** for a musical version of this poem.)

- "King Arthur and His Knights," by Ruth Williams, p. 17 in *Oh, That's Ridiculous,* selected by William Cole, illustrated by Tomi Ungerer. New York: Viking, 1972.

- "La Belle Dame Sans Merci," by John Keats, p. 186 in *A New Treasury of Poetry.*

- "Merlin and the Gleam," by Alfred Tennyson, p. 160 in *A New Treasury of Poetry.*

- "'Night, Night,' Said One Knight," by Anonymous, p. 88 in *Kids Pick the Funniest Poems,* edited by Bruce Lansky, illustrated by Steve Carpenter. New York: Meadowbrook, 1991.

- *The Oxford Book of Children's Verse,* chosen and edited by Iona and Peter Opie. New York & Oxford: Oxford University Press, 1973.

  An entire chapter (pp. 3–17) is devoted to poetry written during the medieval period and the sixteenth century, including "Controlling the Tongue" by Geoffrey Chaucer.

- "Sir Bottomwide," p. 126 in *Something Big Has Been Here,* by Jack Prelutsky, illustrated by James Stevenson. New York: Greenwillow, 1990.

- "Sir Patrick Spens" (traditional), p. 12 in *The Arbuthnot Anthology of Children's Literature* (4th ed., rev.).

- "A Song of Sherwood," by Alfred Noyes, p. 12 in *The Arbuthnot Anthology of Children's Literature* (4th ed., rev.).

- "Unfinished Knews Item," p. 13 in *Chortles: New and Selected Word Play Poems,* by Eve Merriam, illustrated by Sheila Hamanaka. New York: Morrow Junior Books, 1981.

- * "William I—1066," by Eleanor and Herbert Farjeon, p. 52 in *A New Treasury of Poetry.*

- "Young Lochinvar," by Sir Walter Scott, p. 192 in *A New Treasury of Poetry.*

STORIES AND EXCERPTS

- "The Adventure of Countess Jeanne," from *Hero Tales* from *The Age of Chivalry* by Grant Uden, pp. 471–474 in *The Arbuthnot*

Anthology of Children's Literature (4th ed., rev.), selected by May Hill Arbuthnot, Dorothy M. Broderick, Shelton L. Root, Jr., Mark Taylor, and Evelyn L. Wenzel, illustrated by various artists. New York: Lothrop, Lee & Shepard, 1976.

- "Feudalism," pp. 864–866, and "Chivalry," pp. 866–867, from *The Story of Mankind,* by Hendrick Willem Van Loon in *The Arbuthnot Anthology of Children's Literature* (4th ed., rev.). (These two excerpts are informational.)

- "The King and Robert Hood's Horny Beast-es," told by Gaines Kilgore, pp. 50–54 in *American Folk Tales and Songs: And Other Examples of English–American Tradition as Preserved in the Appalachian Mountains and Elsewhere in the United States,* by Richard Chase, illustrated by Joshua Tolford. New York: Dover, 1971.

- "Little John and the Tanner of Blyth," from *The Merry Adventures of Robin Hood,* by Howard Pyle, pp. 460–465 in *The Arbuthnot Anthology of Children's Literature* (4th ed., rev.).

RELATED BOOKS

Fiction

•* Carrick, Donald. *Harald and the Giant Knight,* illustrated by the author. New York: Clarion, 1982. **PJ+**

When a group of rowdy knights uses his father's farm for training, Harald and his family take desperate measures to get them off their land.

•* Carrick, Donald. *Harald and the Great Stag,* illustrated by the author. New York: Clarion, 1988. **PJ+**

Harald comes up with a clever scheme to protect a legendary stag from the Baron and his guests, who plan to hunt the animal.

- Chaucer, Geoffrey. *The Canterbury Tales,* selected, translated, and adapted by Barbara Cohen, illustrated by Trina Schart Hyman. New York: Lothrop, Lee & Shepard, 1988. **J+**

While on their journey, pilgrims entertain each other with stories.

- Chaucer, Geoffrey. *The Canterbury Tales,* retold by Selina Hastings, illustrated by Reg Cartwright. New York: Henry Holt, 1988. **J**

- Chaucer, Geoffrey. *The Canterbury Tales,* [retold by] Geraldine McCaughrean, illustrated by Victor G. Ambrus. Chicago: Rand McNally, 1985. **YA**

- Chaucer, Geoffrey. "Chanticleer and the Fox," adapted from *The Canterbury Tales* by, and illustrated by, Barbara Cooney. New York: HarperCollins, 1989. **PJ+**

- Curry, Jane Louise. *Robin Hood and His Merry Men,* illustrated by John Lytle. New York: Margaret K. McElderry Books/Macmillan, 1994. **J**

- Cushman, Karen. *Catherine, Called Birdy.* New York: Clarion, 1994. **YA**

  The 13-year-old daughter of an English knight records the events of her life in a journal.

- Cushman, Karen. *The Midwife's Apprentice.* New York: Clarion, 1995. **YA**

  A homeless girl finds her place in the world when she is taken in by a sharp-tempered midwife.

- Early, Margaret. *Robin Hood,* illustrated by the author. New York: Abrams, 1996. **PJ+**

- De Angeli, Marguerite. *The Door in the Wall.* New York: Yearling/Dell, 1977. **J**

  A crippled boy proves his courage and earns recognition from the king.

- DePaola, Tomie. *The Knight and the Dragon,* illustrated by the author. New York: Putnam's, 1980. **PJ**

  An inexperienced knight and an inexperienced dragon meet for battle.

- Fox, Paula. *The King's Falcon,* illustrated by Eros Keith. Englewood Cliffs, NJ: Bradbury, 1969. **J**

  A king's dream of freedom comes true because of a falcon.

- Frost, Abigal. *Myths and Legends of the Age of Chivalry,* illustrated by Francis Phillipps. New York: Marshall Cavendish, 1990. **J+**

Includes a chapter on "Chivalry, True and False," which contains information about knights.

- Grahame, Kenneth. *The Reluctant Dragon*, illustrated by Michael Hague. New York: Holt, Rinehart and Winston, 1983. **J**

A boy must convince the villagers and St. George the Dragon Killer not to battle a kindly dragon.

- Gray, Elizabeth Janet. *Adam of the Road*, illustrated by Robert Lawson. New York: Viking, 1970. **J+**

Adam travels the roads of thirteenth-century England searching for his father, who is a minstrel, and his stolen dog.

- Green, Roger Lancelyn. *The Adventures of Robin Hood*, illustrated by Arthur Hall. London: Puffin, 1956. **YA**

- Green, Roger Lancelyn. *King Arthur and His Knights of the Round Table*, illustrated by Aubrey Beardsley. New York: Knopf, 1953, 1993. **J+**

- Greer, Gery, and Bob Ruddick. *Max and Me and the Time Machine*. New York: HarperTrophy, 1983. **J**

Two boys travel in a time machine to the year 1250 and land in the middle of a jousting match.

- Hastings, Selina. *Sir Gawain and the Green Knight*, illustrated by Juan Wijngaard. New York: Lothrop, Lee & Shepard Books, 1981. **J**

Retells the story of Gawain's quest for the Green Chapel.

- Hastings, Selina. *Sir Gawain and the Loathly Lady*, illustrated by Juan Wijngaard. New York: Lothrop, Lee & Shepard, 1985. **J**

See page 128 for description.

- Haugaard, Erik Christian. *Hakon of Rogen's Saga*, illustrated by Leo and Diane Dillon. Boston: Houghton Mifflin/Cambridge: Riverside, 1963. **YA**

A Viking boy, living on an island off the coast of Norway, endures violence and bloodshed while seeking his birthright.

- Hayes, Sarah. *Robin Hood*, illustrated by Patrick Benson. New York: Henry Holt, 1989. **J**

- Heyer, Carol. *Robin Hood,* illustrated by the author. Nashville, TN: Ideals Children's Books, 1993. **PJ+**

- Hodges, Margaret. *The Kitchen Knight,* illustrated by Trina Schart Hyman. New York: Holiday House, 1990. **J**

  Retells the legend of how Sir Gareth becomes a knight and saves the lady imprisoned by the Red Knight.

- Hodges, Margaret. *Saint George and the Dragon* (adapted from Edmund Spenser's *Faerie Queen*), illustrated by Trina Schart Hyman. Boston: Little, Brown, 1984. **J**

  Retells the story about how George, the Red Cross Knight, slays a dragon who terrorized the countryside.

- Howe, John. *The Knight with the Lion: The Story of Yvain,* illustrated by the author. Boston: Little, Brown, 1996. **J**

  Retells the adventures of the knight, Yvain, and his faithful lion.

- Kelly, Eric P. *The Trumpeter of Krakow,* illustrated by Janina Domanska. New York: Macmillan Publishing, 1966. **YA**

  A Polish boy's recollection of a story about a trumpeter of Krakow in earlier times helps him save his father and a secret treasure that his family guards.

- Konigsburg, E. L. *A Proud Taste for Scarlet and Miniver,* illustrated by the author. New York: Yearling/Dell, 1973. **YA**

  Eleanor of Aquitaine reminisces about the events in her life as queen to Louis VII of France and Henry II of England.

- Lister, Robin. *The Story of King Arthur,* illustrated by Alan Baker. New York: Kingfisher, 1997. **J**

- Lofting, Hugh. *The Twilight of Magic,* illustrated by Tatsuro Kiuchi. New York: Simon & Schuster Books for Young Readers, 1993. **J**

  A young boy uses a magic whispering shell to help his young king.

- McCaughrean, Geraldine. *A Little Lower Than the Angels.* Oxford: Oxford University, Press, 1987. **YA**

  Gabriel, a stonemason's apprentice, leaves his abusive master to take the part of an angel in a traveling play.

- McSpadden, J. Walker. *The Adventures of Robin Hood & His Merry Outlaws,* illustrated by Howard Pyle and T. H. Robinson. New York: Greenwich House, 1984. **YA**

- Miles, Bernard. *Robin Hood: His Life and Legend,* illustrated by Victor G. Ambrus. New York: Checkerboard, 1989. **J**

- Mitgutsch, Ali. *A Knight's Book,* illustrated by the author, translated by Elizabeth D. Crawford. New York: Clarion, 1991. **J**

  A young squire relates the adventures of his poor but brave knight participating in a tournament.

- Morpurgo, Michael. *Robin of Sherwood,* illustrated by Michael Foreman. San Diego: Harcourt Brace, 1996. **J+**

- •* Morris, Neil, and Ting Morris. *The Black Knight's Plot,* illustrated by Anna Clarke. Morristown, NJ: Silver Burdett, 1983. **J**

  A young page foils a kidnapping plot and is rewarded by being made a squire.

- O'Dell, Scott. *The Road to Damietta.* New York: Fawcett Juniper/Ballantine, 1985. **YA**

  Attracted to a charming and wealthy youth named Francis, a young noblewoman watches his transformation as he takes a vow of poverty and devotes himself to God. This is a fictional account of St. Francis of Assisi.

- Osborne, Mary Pope. *The Knight at Dawn,* illustrated by Sal Murdocca. New York: A First Stepping Stone Book/Random House, 1993. **PJ**

  A brother and sister travel back in time to a castle in the Middle Ages.

- Pyle, Howard. *Men of Iron,* illustrated by the author. New York: Airmont, 1965. **YA**

  Attempting to avenge his unjustly accused father, a young boy becomes a knight and wins the friendship of King Henry IV.

- Pyle, Howard. *Some Merry Adventures of Robin Hood,* illustrated by the author. New York: Scribner's, 1954. **J**

- Pyle, Howard. *The Story of King Arthur and His Knights,* illustrated by the author. New York: Dover, 1965. **YA**

First volume of four that retells the King Arthur legend. Followed by:

–*The Story of the Champions of the Round Table.* New York: Scribner's, n.d.

–*The Story of Sir Launcelot and His Companions.* New York: Scribner's, 1985.

–*The Story of the Grail and the Passing of Arthur.* New York: Scribner's, n.d.

• Robbins, Ruth. *Taliesin and King Arthur,* illustrated by the author. Berkeley, CA: Parnassus, 1970. **PJ+**

Welsh bard, Taliesin, meets King Arthur.

• Skurzynski, Gloria. *What Happened in Hamelin.* New York: Bullseye/Random House, 1979. **J+**

A retelling of the Pied Piper legend from the perspective of a 14-year-old baker's assistant.

• Strauss, Victoria. *The Lady of Rhuddesmere.* New York: Frederick Warne, 1982. **YA**

Geraint is sent from his father's castle to live in a household where an ancient heresy is practiced.

• Sutcliff, Rosemary. *The Sword and the Circle: King Arthur and the Knights of the Round Table,* illustrated by Shirley Felts. New York: Dutton, 1981. **YA**

This is the first volume of a trilogy retelling the King Arthur legend. Followed by:

–*The Light Beyond the Forest: The Quest for the Holy Grail,* illustrated by Shirley Felts. New York: Dutton, 1980.

–*The Road to Camlann: The Death of Arthur,* illustrated by Shirley Felts. New York: Dutton, 1982.

• Temple, Frances. *The Ramsay Scallop.* New York: Orchard, 1994. **YA**

Set in fourteenth-century England, a girl and her betrothed, a young nobleman, travel together on a pilgrimage to far-off Spain.

• Tripp, Wallace. *Sir Toby Jingle's Beastly Journey,* illustrated by the author. New York: Coward, McCann & Geoghegan, 1976. **PJ**

Brave Sir Toby, goes on one last adventure accompanied by scheming acquaintances.

- Voigt, Cynthia. *Jackaroo.* New York: Argo/Atheneum, 1985. **YA**

  An innkeeper's daughter unlocks the secret behind the legend of the hero Jackaroo.

Nonfiction/Informational

Most of these books include information about the general history of the Middle Ages, the feudal system, the Crusades, castles, knights, chivalry, daily life, religion, culture.

- Aliki. *A Medieval Feast,* illustrated by the author. New York: Crowell, 1983. **J**

- Anno, Mitsumasa. *Anno's Medieval World,* illustrated by the author, translated by Ursula Synge. New York: Philomel, 1979. **J**

  Describes science and navigation in the Middle Ages.

- Berenstain, Michael. *The Castle Book,* illustrated by the author. New York: David McKay, 1977. **J**

- Braun and Schneider. *Historic Costume in Pictures.* New York: Dover, 1975.

  Includes pictures of costumes in the Middle Ages. For adults, but all ages will enjoy looking at the pictures.

- Brochard, Philippe. *Castles of the Middle Ages,* illustrated by Patrice Pellerin, translated by Anthea Ridett. Morristown, NJ: Silver Burdett, 1982. **J**

- Bunson, Matthew. *Encyclopedia of the Middle Ages.* New York: Facts on File, 1995. **YA**

- Burke, John. *Life in the Castle in Medieval England,* illustrations and photographs from various sources. New York: British Heritage Press, 1978. **YA**

- Bushko, Martha. *Costumes for Coloring: Knights & Ladies,* illustrated by Jenny Williams. New York: Grosset & Dunlap, 1996. **J**

- Cairns, Conrad. *Medieval Castles,* illustrations and photographs from various sources. Minneapolis: Lerner Publications, in cooperation with Cambridge University Press, 1989. **J**

- Caselli, Giovanni. *A Medieval Monk,* illustrated by Gino D'Achille. New York: Peter Bedrick, 1986. **J+**

- Caselli, Giovanni. *The Middle Ages,* illustrated by the author. New York: Peter Bedrick, 1988. **J+**

- Caselli, Giovanni. *The Roman Empire and the Dark Ages,* illustrated by the author. New York: Peter Bedrick, 1981. **J+**

- Child, John, Nigel Kelly, and Martyn Whittock. *The Crusades,* illustrated by Jeff Edwards and Douglas Hall, photographs from various sources. New York: Peter Bedrick, 1996. **J**

- Clare, John D., editor. *Knights in Armor,* photographs by Tymn Lyntell (director of photography), Charles Best, and from various other sources. San Diego: Gulliver/Harcourt Brace Jovanovich, 1992. **J**

- Clements, Gillian. *The Truth About Castles,* illustrated by the author. Minneapolis: Carolrhoda, 1990. **J**

- Corbin, Carole Lynn. *Knights,* photographs from various sources. New York: A First Book/Franklin Watts, 1989. **J**

- Corbishley, Mike. *The Medieval World,* illustrated by James Field, photographs from various sources. New York: Peter Bedrick, 1993. **J**

- Corbishley, Mike. *The Middle Ages,* photographs from various sources. New York: Facts on File, 1990. **J+**

- Corrick, James A. *The Early Middle Ages,* illustrated and photographs from various sources. San Diego: Lucent, 1995. **YA**

- Cosman, Madeleine Pelner. *Medieval Holidays and Festivals: A Calendar of Celebrations,* illustrated by various sources. New York: Scribner's, 1981. **J+**

- Dambrosio, Monica, and Roberto Barbieri. *The Early Middle Ages,* illustrated by Remo Berselli and Antonio Molino, translated by Star Language Center. Austin, TX: Raintree Steck-Vaughn, 1992. **YA**

- Day, James. *The Black Death,* illustrated by Patrick Bullock and Peter Bull. New York: Bookwright, 1989. **J**

- Fradon, Dana. *Sir Dana: A Knight, as Told by His Trusty Armor,* illustrated by the author. New York: Dutton, 1988. **J**

- Fradon, Dana. *Harold the Herald: A Book About Heraldry,* illustrated by the author. New York: Dutton Children's Books, 1990. **J**

- Gee, Robyn. *Living in Castle Times,* illustrated by Rob McCaig and Iain Ashman. London: Usborne, 1982. **J**

- Gibbons, Gail. *Knights in Shining Armor,* illustrated by the author. Boston: Little, Brown, 1995. **PJ**

- Goodall, John S. *The Story of a Castle,* illustrated by the author. New York: Macmillan, 1986. **J+**

- Grant, Neil. *The Vikings,* illustrated by various artists. New York: Oxford University Press, 1998. **J**

- Gravett, Christopher. *Castle,* photographs by Geoff Dann. New York: Knopf, 1994. **J**

- Gravett, Christopher. *Knight,* photographs by Geoff Dann. New York: Knopf, 1993. **J**

- Gravett, Christopher. *The Knight's Handbook: How to Become a Champion in Shining Armor,* photographs by David Armstrong. illustrations from various sources. New York: Cobblehill/Dutton, 1997. **J**

- Gregory, Tony. *The Dark Ages,* photographs from various sources. New York: Facts on File, 1993. **J**

- Haaren, John H., and A. B. Poland. *Famous Men of the Middle Ages.* Lebanon, TN: Greenleaf, 1992. **J**

- Hibbert, Christopher. *The Search for King Arthur.* New York: American Heritage, n.d. **YA**

- Hills, Ken. *Crusades,* illustrated by Francis Phillipps. New York: Marshall Cavendish, 1991. **J**

- Howarth, Sarah. *Medieval People,* illustrated by Philip McNeill. Brookfield, CT: Millbrook, 1992. **J**

- Howarth, Sarah. *Medieval Places,* illustrated by Philip McNeill. Brookfield, CT: Millbrook, 1992. **J**

- Howarth, Sarah. *The Middle Ages,* illustrated by various artists. New York: Viking, 1993. **J**

- Hunt, Jonathan. *Illuminations,* illustrated by the author. New York: Bradbury, 1989. **PJ+**

- Langley, Andrew. *Medieval Life,* photographs by Geoff Dann and Geoff Brightling. New York: Knopf, 1996. **J+**

- Lasker, Joe. *Merry Ever After,* illustrated by the author. New York: Viking, 1976. **J+**
  Describes medieval weddings.

- Macaulay, David. *Castle,* illustrated by the author. Boston: Houghton Mifflin, 1977. **J+**

- Macdonald, Fiona. *How Would You Survive in the Middle Ages?* illustrated by Mark Peppe, created and designed by David Salariya. New York: Franklin Watts, 1995. **J**

- Macdonald, Fiona. *A Medieval Castle,* illustrated by Mark Bergin. New York: Peter Bedrick, 1990. **J**

- Macdonald, Fiona. *A Medieval Cathedral,* illustrated by John James. New York: Peter Bedrick, 1994. **J**

- Macdonald, Fiona. *The Middle Ages,* illustrated by Kevin Maddison, Richard Hook, and Ann Baum, photographs from various sources. Morristown, NJ: Silver Burdett, 1985. **J**

- Macdonald, Fiona. *The Middle Ages,* photographs from various sources. New York: Facts on File, 1993. **J**

- Macdonald, Fiona. *A Samurai Castle,* illustrated by John James and David Antram. New York: Peter Bedrick, 1995. **J**

- McNeill, Sarah. *The Middle Ages,* illustrated by various artists. New York: Oxford University Press, 1998. **J**

- Miquel, Pierre. *The Days of Knights & Castles,* illustrated by Pierre Probst, translated by Penny Davies. Morristown, NJ: Silver Burdett, 1981. **J+**

- Monks, John. *The Great Book of Castles,* photographs from various sources. Vero Beach, FL: Rourke, 1989. **J+**

- Morgan, Gwyneth. *Life in a Medieval Village,* illustrations from various sources. Minneapolis: Lerner, 1982. **YA**

- Needham, Kate. *The Time Trekkers Visit the Middle Ages,* illustrated by Sheena Vickers, Ian Thompson, and David Burroughs. Brookfield, CT: Copper Beech, 1996. **PJ**

- Nicolle, David. *Medieval Knights,* illustrated by Bill Donohoe, Terry Gabbey et al. New York: Viking, 1997. **J+**

- Oakes, Catherine. *Exploring the Past: The Middle Ages,* illustrated by Stephen Biesty. San Diego: Gulliver/Harcourt Brace Jovanovich, 1989. **J**

- Osband, Gillian. *Castles: A 3-Dimensional Exploration,* illustrated by Robert Andrew. New York: Orchard, 1991. **ALL AGES**

- Platt, Richard. *Stephen Biesty's Cross-Sections Castle,* illustrated by Stephen Biesty. New York: Dorling Kindersley, 1994. **J+**

- Powell, Anton. *The Rise of Islam,* illustrated by Nigel Chamberlain and Richard Hook, photographs from various sources. New York: Warwick, 1980. **J**

- Ross, Stewart. *A Crusading Knight,* illustrated by Mark Bergin. Vero Beach, FL: Rourke, 1987. **J**

- Rutland, Jonathan. *Knights and Castles,* illustrated by various artists. New York: Random House, 1987. **J**

- Sancha, Sheila. *The Luttrell Village,* illustrated by the author. New York: Crowell, 1982. **J+**

- Sancha, Sheila. *Walter Dragun's Town,* illustrated by the author. New York: Crowell, 1989. **J+**

- Schnurnberger, Lynn Edelman. *Kings, Queens, Knights & Jesters: Making Medieval Costumes,* illustrated by Alan Robert Showe, photographs by Barbara Brooks and Pamela Hort. New York: Harper & Row, 1978. **J+**

- Smith, Beth. *Castles,* illustrated by Anne Canevari Green, photographs from various sources. New York: A First Book/Franklin Watts, 1988. **J**

- Steel, Anne, and Barry Steel. *The Normans,* illustrated by Gerry Wood. Vero Beach, FL: Rourke, 1987. **J**

- Steele, Philip. *Castles,* illustrated by various artists, photographs from various sources. New York: Kingfisher, 1995. **J**

- *Ultimate Castle & Knight Sticker Book, The.* New York: DK Publishing, 1997. **PJ**

- Unstead, R. J. *Living in a Crusader Land,* illustrated by Victor Ambrus. London: A. & C. Black/Reading, MA: Addison-Wesley, 1971. **J**

- Unstead, R. J. *Living in a Medieval City,* illustrated by Ron Stenberg. London: A. & C. Black/Reading, MA: Addison-Wesley, 1971. **J**

- Unstead, R. J. *Living in a Medieval Village,* illustrated by Ron Stenberg. London: A. & C. Black/Reading, MA: Addison-Wesley, 1971. **J**

- Windrow, Martin. *The Medieval Knight,* illustrated by Richard Hook. New York: Franklin Watts, 1985. **J**

- Wright, Rachel. *Castles,* illustrated by Jeremy Semmens, photographs by Chris Fairclough. New York: Franklin Watts, 1992. **J**

- Wright, Rachel. *Knights,* illustrated by Ed Dovey, photographs from various sources. New York: Franklin Watts, 1991. **J**

- Wright, Rachel. *The Viking News,* illustrated by various artists. New York: Franklin Watts, 1991. **J**

Additional Ideas
for Guest Readers
and Read-Alouds

Alternative read-aloud materials might be included under several of the listings for one or more of the following reasons: To provide a backup read-aloud in case you are unable to find the first recommendation; to provide options that might be more age-appropriate for your group; to offer different types of formats for variety or because the alternate is equally as good as the primary suggestion. Also listed are a few ideas for discussion topics/demonstrations and follow-up activities.

GUEST READER: ACTOR

Read-Aloud: Amazing Grace, by Mary Hoffman, illustrated by Caroline Binch. New York: Dial Books for Young Readers, 1991.

Alternative Read-Aloud: "The Lovely Desdemona," pp. 149–150 in *Destiny,* by Paul Aurandt. New York: Morrow, 1983.

Discussion Topics/Demo: Job description and training; job opportunities; differences between acting on screen and on stage; voice-overs. Demonstrate different interpretations of the same speech. Ask student volunteers to say "thank you" as if they are sad, surprised, angry, sincere, etc.

Follow-Up Activities: Play theater games; act out scenes or plays.

GUEST READER: ARTIST

Read-Aloud: The Art Lesson, by Tomie dePaola, illustrated by the author. New York: Putnam's, 1989.

Alternative Read-Alouds:

- *The Artist,* by John Bianchi, illustrated by the author. Newburgh, ON, Canada: Bungalo/Buffalo, NY: Firefly, 1993.
- *Matthew's Dream,* by Leo Lionni, illustrated by the author. New York: Knopf, 1991.
- *Painting the Wind,* by Michelle Dionetti, illustrated by Kevin Hawkes. Boston: Little, Brown, 1996.

Discussion Topics/Demo: Job description and training; job opportunities; explanation of the "tools of the trade." Show the process of creating art in whatever medium the Guest Reader is an expert. (Our Guest Reader was an illustrator and demonstrated his skills while giving tips on drawing to the students.)

Follow-Up Activities: Write and illustrate an autobiographical picture book. Use *The Art Lesson* by Tomie dePaola as an example.

GUEST READER: ASTRONOMER

Read-Aloud: Alistair in Outer Space, by Marilyn Sadler, illustrated by Roger Bollen. New York: Simon & Schuster, 1984.

Alternative Read-Alouds:

- *Keepers of the Earth: Native American Stories and Environmental Activities for Children,* by Michael J. Caduto and Joseph Bruchac, illustrated by John Kahionhes Fadden and Carol Wood. Golden, CO: Fulcrum, 1989.

  Choose one of the legends about the sun, moon, stars, etc.

- *Sky Songs,* by Myra Cohn Livingston, illustrated by Leonard Everett Fisher. New York: Holiday House, 1984.

Choose one or two of the poems, such as "Moon," p. 5; "Stars," p. 7; "The Planets," p. 9; "Shooting Stars," p. 11.

- *Spaceways: An Anthology of Space Poems,* selected by John Foster, illustrated by many artists. Oxford: Oxford University Press, 1986.

    Choose one or two of the poems, such as "I Am . . . Star Counting," by John Rice, p. 8; "Planets," by Jean Kenward, p. 60; "The Planets Turn In Stately Dance," by John Kitching, p. 61.

Discussion Topics/Demo: Job description and training; solar system; eclipses; space program. Show photographs from outer space and a telescope. (We looked at the sun through a special telescope brought by our Guest Reader from the Los Angeles Griffith Observatory.)

Follow-Up Activities: Create a model of the solar system. Write legends about the solar system.

GUEST READER: AUTHOR

Read-Aloud: An excerpt from one of the author's works.

Alternative Read-Alouds:

- "Feelings About Words," by Mary O'Neill, p. 197, and "A Word," by Emily Dickinson, p. 196, in *The Random House Book of Poetry for Children,* selected by Jack Prelutsky, illustrated by Arnold Lobel. New York: Random House, 1983.

- "I Love the Look of Words," by Maya Angelou (no pagination) in *Soul Looks Back in Wonder,* illustrated by Tom Feelings. New York: Dial, 1993.

- "Kingdom in a File Drawer," pp. 242–244 in *Destiny,* by Paul Aurandt. New York: Morrow, 1983.

Discussion Topics/Demo: Explanation of the writing process, including how writers get their inspiration, how they must rewrite and edit, etc. (Our Guest Reader showed galleys and mock-ups of her books. She also encouraged students to not only write stories and poems, but to hone their skills by keeping a journal and by writing letters.)

Follow-Up Activities: Play "add-a-line"—each students adds a line to a story; keep journals; write letters, poems, stories, essays, books.

GUEST READER: CHARACTER EDUCATION TEACHER/ ETHICS TEACHER

Read-Aloud: Teammates, by Peter Golenbock, illustrated by Paul Bacon. San Diego: Harcourt Brace Jovanovich, 1990.

Discussion Topics/Demo: Tolerance and treating others with decency; causes of prejudice; the consequences of hurting others; courage to stand up for what is right. Present hypothetical situations and ask the students how they would handle themselves. (These topics relate to the theme of the read-aloud book. Choose another read-aloud if your Guest Reader wishes to discuss other issues, for example, honesty.)

Follow-Up Activities: Discuss current events that relate to the topic; write a true story about how they were hurt by someone or how they hurt someone else (change names for privacy); write about a time they showed courage; write about famous courageous people; write fictional stories about the topic; list ways to become a kinder person.

GUEST READER: CHEMIST

Read-Aloud: What Are Scientists? What Do They Do? Let's Find Out, by Rita Golden Gleman and Susan Kovacs Buxbaum, illustrated by Mark Teague. New York: Scholastic, 1991.

Alternative Read-Alouds:
- *The A,B,C of the Biosphere,* by Professor Finch, illustrated by Mary Beath. Oracle, AZ: Biosphere, 1993.

Choose one or two of the poems about the elements, such as "H is for Hydrogen."

- "Aspirin," pp. 26–28, or "Penicillin," pp. 30–32 in *Mistakes That Worked,* by Charlotte Foltz Jones, illustrated by John O'Brien. New York: Doubleday, 1991.

- "I Made Something Strange with My Chemistry Set," p. 58 in *A Pizza the Size of the Sun,* by Jack Prelutsky, illustrated by James Stevenson. New York: Greenwillow, 1996.

Discussion Topics/Demo: Job description and training; job opportunities; scientific method. (Our Guest Readers gave the students a wrapped box and asked them to determine what was inside by using the scientific method.) Perform experiments.

Follow-Up Activities: Perform experiments. (Our Guest Readers gave the students directions for an experiment to do at home. They returned the next day to discuss the results with the classes.)

GUEST READER: CIVIL WAR RE-ENACTOR/HISTORIAN

Read-Aloud: Follow the Drinking Gourd, by Jeanette Winter, illustrated by the author. New York: Knopf, 1988.

Alternative Read-Alouds:

- "Get Those Shoes," pp. 56–58 in *Destiny,* by Paul Aurandt. New York: Morrow, 1983.

The first Civil War Re-enactor I invited to be a Guest Reader read *Follow the Drinking Gourd,* about the underground railroad. The Guest Reader explained that the conflict over slavery was one of the causes of the Civil War. A few years later, another re-enactor appeared as Guest Reader. He had a different approach and intertwined the following excerpts into his presentation:

- *Civil War Curiosities,* by Webb Garrison. Nashville, TN: Rutledge Hill, 1994, p. 218.

Gives a description of Abraham Lincoln.

- *Civil War Handbook,* by William H. Price. Fairfax, VA: Prince, 1961, p. 5.

  Lists "firsts" that occurred during the Civil War.

- *Don't Know Much About the Civil War: Everything You Need to Know About America's Greatest Conflict But Never Learned,* by Kenneth C. Davis. New York: Morrow, 1996, p. 186.

  Describes Beauregard's call to war. The Guest Reader used this to explain why "he enlisted."

Discussion Topics/Demo: Our Guest Readers were Civil War Re-enactors who discussed the causes of the Civil War, the life of a soldier, described a few famous battles, and showed artifacts from the era, while they were "in character."

Follow-Up Activities: Adapt the ideas presented in Program Plan V.

GUEST READER: DETECTIVE

Read-Aloud: "The Road Through Rushton Forest," pp. 82–86 in *The Castle of the Red Gorillas,* by Wolfgang Ecke, illustrated by Rolf Rettich, translated from the German by Stella and Vernon Humphries. Englewood Cliffs, NJ: Prentice-Hall, 1983.

  The students help solve the mystery. The solution is given at the end.

Alternative Read-Alouds: There are many collections of mini-mysteries, like the one recommended above, that are available where the children are given clues throughout the story and then they must solve the mystery. The solutions are usually given at the end of the book.

- "We Never Sleep," pp. 136–138 in *Destiny* by Paul Aurandt. New York: Morrow, 1983.

  This is a story about Allan Pinkerton.

Discussion Topics/Demo: Job description and training; description of methods for gathering clues and solving crimes; forensic science; tips on how to avoid being a victim. (Our Guest Reader also discussed the cases he worked on and presented a strong antidrug and antigang message.) See above for description of the demo.

Follow-Up Activities: Discuss current cases appearing in the news; write mysteries, present them to the class and ask the class to guess "whodunit."

GUEST READER: DIETITIAN (REGISTERED)

Read-Aloud: Gregory, the Terrible Eater, by Mitchell Sharmat, illustrated by Jose Aruego and Ariane Dewey. New York: Four Winds/Macmillan, 1980.

Alternative Read-Alouds:

- "The Cracker That Was Banned in Boston: Graham Cracker," pp. 11–16 in *The Rejects: People and Products that Outsmarted the Experts,* by Nathan Aaseng, illustrations and photographs from various sources. Minneapolis: Lerner, 1989.

  This must be condensed.

- "In the Pantry," by Charles Panati, pp. 448–455 in *Read All About It!: Great Read-Aloud Stories, Poems, & Newspaper Pieces For Preteens and Teens,* edited by Jim Trelease. New York: Penguin, 1993.

  Choose one or two of the stories that describe the origin of snacks such as popcorn.

- "Tummy Fillers" section, pp. 1–25, in *Mistakes That Worked,* by Charlotte Foltz Jones, illustrated by John O'Brien. New York: Doubleday, 1991.

  Choose one or two of the stories that describe snacks that were "invented" by mistake such as the sandwich and chocolate-chip cookie. If this Read-Aloud is used, the Guest Reader might challenge the students to develop or "invent" nutritious snacks.

Discussion Topics/Demo: Job description and training; importance of diet and exercise; explanation of how food affects our health.

Follow-Up Activities: Keep a diary of personal nutrition and diet. Try new recipes for nutritious meals. Create a menu with healthy foods. Discuss news reports that relate to the topic.

GUEST READER: ENTOMOLOGIST

Read-Aloud: Anansi Goes Fishing, retold by Eric A. Kimmel, illustrated by Janet Stevens. New York: Holiday House, 1992.

Even though a spider is not technically an insect, it is still a crawly creature! In addition, this story gave the Guest Reader a perfect opportunity to explain the difference between an insect and an arachnid before he presented his insect zoo that he brought from the Museum of Natural History.

Alternative Read-Alouds:

- *Anansi and the Moss-Covered Rock,* retold by Eric A. Kimmel, illustrated by Janet Stevens. New York: Holiday House, 1988.

- *Someone Saw a Spider: Spider Facts and Folktales,* by Shirley Climo, illustrated by Dirk Zimmer. New York: Crowell, 1985.

  Choose one of the stories.

- *Insects: Over 300 Fun Facts for Curious Kids,* by Molly Marr, illustrated by Paul Mirocha. New York: A Golden Book, 1992.

  Read a few facts from the "Amazing But True" sections.

Discussion Topics/Demo: Job description and training; habits of insects; metamorphosis; camouflage; how insects are important to the environment and humans. (Our Guest Reader also described and showed us various insects in his "zoo.")

Follow-Up Activities: Write a report about an insect; create a new legend about Anansi or write a legend about an insect; write a story/fantasy about insects à la *James and the Giant Peach,* by Ronald Dahl; create models of bugs and insect mobiles.

GUEST READER: ETIQUETTE EXPERT

Read-Aloud: Monster Manners, by Joanna Cole, illustrated by Jared Lee. New York: Scholastic, 1985.

Discussion Topics/Demo: Basic rules of etiquette; explanation of why manners are important. Have students participate in skits demonstrating proper telephone etiquette, introductions, etc.

Follow-Up Activities: Create skits demonstrating proper etiquette; write a manners book; have a formal dinner as a class event.

GUEST READER: GUIDE DOG TRAINER AND/OR A PERSON WHO IS BLIND

Read-Aloud: Mom Can't See Me, by Sally Hobart Alexander, photographs by George Ancona. New York: Macmillan /London: Collier Macmillan, 1990.

Alternative Read-Aloud: "Dog Guides for Blind People," pp. 28–30 in Mistakes That Worked, by Charlotte Foltz Jones, illustrated by John O'Brien. New York: Doubleday, 1991.

Discussion Topics/Demo: Blindness and its causes; how to protect the eyes; Braille; the Braille Institute; how to interact with a blind person; training of guide dogs and how they help blind people. (Our Guest Reader brought a guide dog with her to help with the demonstration, and she showed a short video.)

Follow-Up Activities: Blindfolded, use the other senses to guess what various items are. Write a report about Louis Braille, Helen Keller, and other famous blind people.

GUEST READER: GYMNAST/GYMNASTICS COACH

Read-Aloud: Angelina and Alice, by Katharine Holabird, illustrated by Helen Craig. New York: Clarkson Potter, 1987.

Alternative Read-Aloud: "The Gymnasts," by Irving Feldman, p. 170, and "Uneven Parallel Bars," by Patricia Gary, p. 171, in *American Sports Poems,* selected by R. R. Knudson and May Swenson. New York: Orchard, 1988.

Discussion Topics/Demo: Training; equipment; events. (Gymnasts performed for the classes while our Guest Reader provided narration.)

Follow-Up Activities: Watch gymnastic events and write "sports articles" describing them; read articles about gymnastics; write a report about a prominent gymnast; participate in gymnastics, but only with a trained coach. Also, adapt the ideas presented in Program Plan II.

GUEST READER: INTERPRETER FOR THE DEAF AND/OR A PERSON WHO IS DEAF

Read-Aloud: Words in Our Hand, by Ada B. Litchfield, illustrated by Helen Cogancherry. Chicago: Albert Whitman, 1980.

Alternative Read-Alouds:

- "Bell's Belles," pp. 229–230 in *Paul Harvey's the Rest of the Story,* by Paul Aurandt. Garden City, NY: Doubleday, 1977.

- *I Have a Sister, My Sister Is Deaf,* by Jeanne Whitehouse Peterson, illustrated by Deborah Ray. New York: Harper & Row, 1977.

Discussion Topics/Demo: Deafness and causes; devices that help the deaf community; methods of communication, for example, the American Sign Language. (Our Guest Readers, a deaf woman and an interpreter, taught the students to sign a simple song.)

Follow-Up Activities: Discuss the many ways people communicate without using words; learn American Sign Language; write a report about a prominent deaf person: write about Alexander Graham Bell; Ludwig van Beethoven; Marlee Matlin (actress who starred in *Children of a Lesser God*).

GUEST READER: INVENTOR

Read-Aloud: *Alistair's Time Machine,* by Marilyn Sadler, illustrated by Roger Bollen. New York: Simon & Schuster, 1986.

The Guest Reader introduced the book by saying it is frustrating when an invention works in the laboratory but fails when demonstrated for the public, which is what happens to Alistair!

Alternative Read-Alouds:

- "And Yet Fools Say," by George S. Holmes, p. 32 in *The Arbuthnot Anthology of Children's Literature,* by May Hill Arbuthnot, Dorothy M. Broderick, Shelton L. Root, Jr., Mark Taylor, and Evelyn L. Wenzel, illustrated by various artists. New York: Lothrop, Lee & Shepard, 1976.

- "The Genius of Karl Kroyer," pp. 130–133 in *Destiny* by Paul Aurandt. New York: Morrow, 1983.

- "The Misfortunes of Mahlon Loomis," pp. 209–210 in *Destiny.*

Choose one or two stories from one of the following books:

- *Discovery & Inventions,* by Geoff Endacott, photographs from various sources. New York: Viking, 1991.

- *53½ Things That Changed the World and Some That Didn't,* by Steve Parker, illustrated by David West. Brookfield, CT: Millbrook, 1992.

- *Mistakes That Worked,* by Charlotte Foltz Jones, illustrated by John O'Brien. New York: Doubleday, 1991.

Choose a story from one of the following books written by Nathan Aaseng. They will need to be condensed:

- *Better Mousetraps: Product Improvements That Led to Success,* photographs from various sources. Minneapolis: Lerner, 1990.

- *The Problem Solvers: People Who Turned Problems into Products,* illustrations and photographs from various sources. Minneapolis: Lerner, 1989.

- *The Rejects: People and Products That Outsmarted the Experts,* illustrations and photographs from various sources. Minneapolis: Lerner, 1989.

- *The Unsung Heroes,* photographs from various sources. Minneapolis: Lerner Publications, 1989.

Discussion Topics/Demo: Famous inventors, including female inventors and inventors from various ethnic groups; children inventors; how inventions impact our lives; most recent inventions; the patent process; how to become an inventor; invention contests. (Our Guest Reader demonstrated his own inventions and challenged the students to develop ones of their own. One young girl was so inspired by the Guest Reader that she showed him a design for one of her ideas. He invited her to appear on a local television program with him to talk about her invention!)

Follow-Up Activities: Write a story about an invention; write a report about inventors and inventions; create an invention; describe how an invention personally affected their life; predict future inventions.

GUEST READER: JUDGE OR ATTORNEY

Read-Aloud: The Wise Fool, adapted and illustrated by Paul Galdone. Toronto, ON, Canada: Pantheon/New York: Random House, 1968.

Alternative Read-Aloud: You Be the Judge, by Sidney B. Carroll, illustrated by John Richmond. New York: Lothrop, Lee & Shepard, 1971.

The cases in this book are based on real cases. Choose one or two to read; then the students should come up with a decision. The real verdict is provided. This book is an entertaining way to involve the class. If there is time, ask the Guest Reader to read both read-alouds; or you may wish the Guest Reader to only read from *You Be the Judge.*

Alternative Read-Aloud for an Attorney: "The Outcasts," pp. 256–257 in *Destiny,* by Paul Aurandt. New York: Morrow, 1983.

This is a negative story, but interesting! Create an introduction to mitigate any negativity.

Discussion Topics/Demo: Job description and training; discussion of the differences between civil and criminal trials; description of the court system (namely: municipal, superior, appellate, U.S.

Supreme Court); a judge's responsibilities; reason for wearing black robe. See above for description of demo. If the Guest Reader is an attorney, discuss different types of lawyers, for example, criminal lawyer, corporate lawyer.

Follow-Up Activities: Analyze trials in the news; discuss famous trials throughout history; discuss recent Supreme Court decisions; present a mock trial.

GUEST READER: LAWMAKER

Read-Aloud: "The Kingdom with No Rules, No Laws, and No Kings," by Norman Stiles, illustrated by Arnie Levin, pp. 142–147 in *Free to Be . . . Family,* conceived and edited by Marlo Thomas, illustrated by various artists. New York: Bantam, 1987.
   This needs to be condensed.

Discussion Topics/Demo: Job description; consequences of having no laws; government structure and legislature; legislative process (include information about a specific law that will directly affect the students); discussion of how to be a good citizen; discussion of how to solve community/state/national problems.

Follow-Up Activities: Talk about bills and laws discussed in the news; write about famous lawmakers; learn about the Constitution; form a student government and pass class rules.

GUEST READER: MAKEUP ARTIST

Read-Aloud: Miss Rumphius, by Barbara Cooney, illustrated by the author. New York: Puffin, 1987.
   This needs to be condensed. Also, the story has nothing to do with being a makeup artist! It traces the life of an adventurous woman from early girlhood until she is very old. We used this book because our Guest Reader asked a young girl [a young boy could also volunteer] to serve as a model. The Makeup Artist then aged

the student using stage makeup. Thus, like Miss Rumphius, who ages in the book, the young student also ages before our eyes! Remember to get a volunteer and backup volunteer(s) days in advanced and ask their parents to sign a permission slip.

Discussion Topics/Demo: Job description and training; reason why actors need to wear makeup on screen and on stage; "tools of the trade," for example, wigs; how to create visual effects, for example, blood. See above for a description of the demo.

Follow-Up Activities: Using makeup, create characters, such as monsters and clowns. Talk about television shows or movies that use unusual makeup to create effects.

GUEST READER: METEOROLOGIST

Read-Aloud: Cloudy with a Chance of Meatballs, by Judi Barrett, illustrated by Ron Barrett. New York: Macmillan, 1978.

Alternative Read-Alouds:

- There are many wonderful poems about the weather in anthologies, such as in *The Random House Book of Poetry for Children*, selected by Jack Prelutsky, illustrated by Arnold Lobel. New York: Random House, 1983.

- *Can It Really Rain Frogs?: The World's Strangest Weather Events*, by Spencer Christian and Antonia Felix, illustrated by Abe Blashko and Jessica Wolk-Stanley. New York: Wiley, 1997.

  Choose one or two stories to read such as "Raining Snakes, Frogs and Fish," p. 28, or "The Famous Weather-Forecasting Goats of Mt. Nebo," p. 91.

- *Tales of Thunder and Lightning*, by Harry Devlin, illustrated by the author. New York: Parents' Magazine Press, 1975.

  Choose one or two stories to read.

Discussion Topics/Demo: Job description and training; presentation and explanation of weather instruments, for example, barometer; description of newest ways to predict weather, for example, satellites; safety tips for protection from lightening, etc.; nature's weathermen, for example, counting cricket chirps to determine temperature; history of forecasting; conduct weather experiments.

Follow-Up Activities: Track daily temperature and create a graph; draw pictures and write poems about the weather; conduct weather experiments.

GUEST READER: NATIVE AMERICAN (OR A REPRESEN-TATIVE OF A DIFFERENT CULTURE)

Read-Aloud: Dancing with the Indians, by Angela Shelf Medearis, illustrated by Samuel Byrd. New York: Holiday House, 1991.

Alternative Read-Alouds: Choose an American Indian tale from one of these books:

- *From Sea to Shining Sea: A Treasury of American Folklore and Folk Songs,* compiled by Amy L. Cohn, illustrated by various artists. New York: Scholastic, 1993.

- *Keepers of the Earth: Native American Stories and Environmental Activities for Children,* by Michael J. Caduto and Joseph Bruchac, illustrated by John Kahionhes Fadden and Carol Wood. Golden, CO: Fulcrum, 1989.

Discussion Topics/Demo: Explanation of clothes, jewelry, instruments, and other artifacts; brief description of history, for example, the Seminole Wars; impact on United States history, for example, the U.S. Constitution is based on the Iroquois Constitution; respect for the Earth's environment. (Our Guest Reader taught us a Friendship Dance, danced in a circle.)

Follow-Up Activities: Write a report about a tribe; discuss the history of Native Americans and how they have been treated; talk about issues that appear in the news.

GUEST READER: OPTOMETRIST

Read-Aloud: *Arthur's Eyes,* by Marc Brown, illustrated by the author. Boston: An Atlantic Monthly Press Book/Little, Brown, 1979.

Alternative Read-Alouds:

- A description of the invention of glasses can be found in *Discovery & Inventions,* by Geoff Endacott, photographs from various sources. New York: Viking, 1991, p. 66.

- *Fenton's Leap,* by Libba Moore Gray, illustrated by Jo-Ellen Bosson. New York: Simon & Schuster Books for Young Readers, 1994.

Discussion Topics/Demo: Job description and training; description of eye exam; presentation of equipment; advancements in correcting vision; how to protect the eyes. Younger children will enjoy trying frames on! All students enjoy looking at a model of an eye.

GUEST READER: PSYCHOLOGIST

Read-Aloud: *Alexander and the Terrible, Horrible, No Good, Very Bad Day,* by Judith Viorst, illustrated by Ray Cruz. New York: Atheneum, 1972.

Alternative Read-Alouds:

- "I Should Have Stayed in Bed Today," p. 28 in *Something Big Has Been Here,* by Jack Prelutsky, illustrated by James Stevenson. New York: Greenwillow, 1990.

- "Why?," by Myra Cohn Livingston, p. 72, and "Hurt," by Marcie Hans, p. 73, in *Celebrating America: A Collection of Poems and Images of the American Spirit,* compiled by Laura Whipple, art provided by the Art Institute of Chicago. New York: Philomel Books, in association with the Art Institute of Chicago, 1994.

Discussion Topics/Demo: Job description and training; presentation of a "How I Feel Today" poster; discussion of how to deal with emotions; presentation of "tools of the trade," for example, interpretative cards; discussion of typical problems for age group.

Follow-Up Activities: Write a poem, story, or essay on how to deal with sad or angry feelings; write a report about the history of psychiatry.

GUEST READER: QUILTER

Read-Aloud: The Quilt Story, by Tony Johnston, illustrated by Tomie dePaola. New York: Putnam's, 1985.

Alternative Read-Alouds:

- *The Keeping Quilt,* by Patricia Polacco, illustrated by the author. New York: Simon & Schuster Books for Young Readers, 1988.

- *The Patchwork Quilt,* by Valerie Flournoy, illustrated by Jerry Pinkney. New York: Dial Books for Young Readers, 1985.

- *Sweet Clara and the Freedom Quilt,* by Deborah Hopkinson, illustrated by James Ransome. New York: Knopf, 1993.

Discussion Topics/Demo: History and purpose of quilts; type of quilting, for example, wadded and flat; quilting designs and patterns; simple ways to create quilts. (Our Guest Reader showed a quilt that she and a group of women created with scenes representing the history of our town. Not only did the students learn about quilts, they also learned about the history of our community!)

GUEST READER: TELEVISION PRODUCER

Read-Aloud: The Bionic Bunny Show, by Marc Brown and Laurene Krasny Brown, illustrated by Marc Brown. Boston: Little, Brown, 1984.

Alternative Read-Aloud: Use an excerpt of a script from the Television Producer's show. Provide a script for each student and ask student volunteers to take parts and read from the script.

Discussion Topics/Demo: Job description; description of key members of production staff; explanation of terms; explanation of how scenes are set up and shot. (Our Guest Reader brought in props, masks, costumes from his *Star Trek* series!)

GUEST READER: TRACK COACH AND/OR TRACK TEAM MEMBER

Read-Aloud: *Wilma Unlimited: How Wilma Rudolph Became the World's Fastest Woman,* by Kathleen Krull, illustrated by David Diaz. San Diego: Harcourt, Brace, 1996.

Alternative Read-Alouds:

- "Atalanta," by Betty Miles, illustrated by Barbara Bascove, pp. 128–135 in *Free to Be . . . You and Me,* conceived by Marlo Thomas, illustrated by various artists. New York: McGraw-Hill, 1974.

- "The Power of Determination," by Burt Dubin, pp. 259–260 in *Chicken Soup for the Soul: 101 Stories to Open the Heart & Rekindle the Spirit,* written and compiled by Jack Canfield and Mark Victor Hansen. Deerfield Beach, FL: Health, 1993.

  This can also be found in *Chicken Soup for the Teenage Soul: 101 Stories of Life, Love and Learning,* by Jack Canfield, Mark Victor Hansen, and Kimberly Kirberger (Deerfield Beach, FL: Health, 1997), pp. 321–322, under the title "From Crutches To a World-Class Runner."

- *The Tortoise and the Hare* (An Aesop Fable), adapted by Janet Stevens, illustrated by the author. New York: Holiday House, 1984.

Discussion Topics/Demo: Training; how to start a personal running program; importance of a warmup and cooldown; importance of good running shoes; how to run properly; various track events. (Our Guest Reader showed a short video describing the different events. After his talk, the Guest Reader organized a relay race with the students.)

Follow-Up Activities: Adapt the ideas presented in Program Plan II.

GUEST READER: VOTER REGISTRATION OFFICIAL

Read-Aloud: Use a current article about candidates. Our Guest Reader visited during a Presidential campaign. He read a selection about the candidates' childhoods that appeared in a special *Newsweek* issue that was geared towards young people. It was a perfect choice because it was "immediate," and as one teacher wrote to me: "The article modeled for the children that they can find useful, interesting material from other sources."

Alternative Read-Alouds:

- *The Day Gogo Went to Vote,* by Elinor Batezat Sisulu, illustrated by Sharon Wilson. Boston: Little, Brown, 1996.

- An excerpt about Edmund Ross, pp. 74–78 in *Encyclopedia of Presidents: Andrew Johnson,* by Zachary Kent, photographs from various sources. Chicago: Childrens Press, 1989.

  This needs to be condensed.

- "The First Woman To Vote In the State of California," by Carolyn Polese, illustrated by Barbara Cooney, pp. 182–185 in *From Sea to Shining Sea: A Treasury of American Folklore and Folk Songs,* compiled by Amy L. Cohn, illustrated by various artists. New York: Scholastic, 1993.

  This needs to be condensed.

Discussion Topics/Demo: Brief history of voting in the United States; explanation of the Electoral College; the importance of voting; voting requirements and process. (Our Guest Reader showed the class a ballot, then the students went into the voting booth the Guest Reader brought with him and cast their "votes" for the candidates! One of the students was so impressed by this presentation, he begged his mother, who was born in another country, to become a citizen so that she could have a voice in our government. And she did!)

Follow-Up Activities: Study different types of governments and how their leaders are chosen; discuss elections covered in the news; vote for class officers; work on a campaign.

Conclusion

Guest Readers give students a view of the world beyond the classroom. They show how academics fit into the context of "real" life, thus making schoolwork more meaningful. They inspire young people to read and learn about new things. The Guest Readers Program is an excellent example of how schools in partnership with the community can positively impact children's lives.

I have seen the excitement the Guest Readers Program generates. Universally, those involved have found their experience to be both unique and rewarding. In this final chapter, librarians, educators, students, and Guest Readers share their thoughts.

LIBRARIANS

"After a Guest Reader's presentation at the local school, the children would come into the library looking for books about the Reader's topic. The children viewed careers as something to learn more about. A career was no longer just a job that they would seek someday in the future. Careers became real to the students."

LINDA CAPICOTTO
Children's Librarian
Chatsworth Branch
Los Angeles Public Library

"We always knew the day it was 'Guest Readers' because that afternoon we would be deluged with students asking for books they were exposed to at school. The Guest Readers Program is a wonderful way to introduce children to various occupations, and we saw the enthusiasm carry over to the library as the students wanted to read more about it. Adrienne Anderson did a remarkable job putting the program together.

BRUCE SEIDMAN
Senior Librarian
Chatsworth Branch
Los Angeles Public Library

EDUCATORS

"The class of 2000—what dreams these students have! Many of these dreams were instilled when the students were fifth graders—as a result of the Guest Readers Program. Our class experienced the Civil War and became historians, looked through a special telescope at the sun and followed *Alistair In Outer Space* and became astronomers, and *Dancing With the Indians* we circled round to Native American rhythms. We became knowledgeable citizens—learned about the presidential candidates and voting, and we were inspired to be the best we could be through character education. My students realized and verbalized that they will impact the world. As I surveyed the books my students were reading, I saw the Guest Readers selections used time and time again. This is an incredibly motivating program, and I feel privileged to have been a part of it."

MARY DAPAS
Fifth Grade Teacher
Germain Street School
Chatsworth, CA

"The Guest Readers Program is an outstanding way to motivate students of all ages. These visitors can make the events and personalities on the written page suddenly come alive. Whether used at the onset of a particular area of study or as a culmination, the Guest Readers Program is a valuable learning tool."

RUSTY KAMAN
English Department
Lawrence Middle School
Chatsworth, CA

"The Guest Readers Program is wonderful! During our Middle Ages unit, the Medieval History interpreters added a new dimension to our learning. Students got a different perspective of the knights after seeing the armor they wore. The students could not get enough. The story that was read was exactly what my students needed to get the flavor of the time period. With the newspaper editor, students heard about the importance of writing and what careers were available to those who enjoy writing. The Guest Readers Program was a hit! The experience the students got could not have been obtained from a textbook. It was a 'real' experience."

KATHY MOSLEY
Humanities Teacher
Medea Creek Middle School
Oak Park, CA

"The Guest Readers Program was a bright light at our school. Students were inspired by the Guest Readers. For these children, reading and careers came alive. Nothing is more important than encouraging students to read. This program merges real life with children's literature. The Guest Readers Program is a win–win for everyone!"

BRENDA WINTER
Assistant Principal
Lawrence Middle School
Chatsworth, CA

STUDENTS

"The Guest Readers Program enriched my life by exposing me to people who are employed in various occupations. It showed jobs available to me in the future and the qualifications I need to achieve in the real world."

JORDAN LEVINE (14 years old)
Chatsworth, CA

"The Guest Readers were always a lot of fun. They actually *taught* us while keeping us entertained at the same time. I remember that after each Guest Reader, I wanted to learn more about their line of work and to read more books that were linked to their subject."

BLAIR ANDERSON (14 years old)
Oak Park, CA

GUEST READERS

"I recall the remarkable interest and attention the kids had in the story I was reading. And as a Reader, the experience gave me a new perspective—to get out of the office of *Star Trek: The Next Generation* and into the community to actually *meet* the next generation. It serves to remind what we're all here to do—to prepare our kids for the future."

MICHAEL PILLER
Creator/Creative Consultant /Executive Producer of *Star Trek: Deep Space Nine* and *Star Trek: Voyager*.
Executive Producer of *Star Trek: The Next Generation*

"Appearing as a Guest Reader gave me the opportunity to encourage the children to read. I reminded them that they spend twenty-four hours a day with the same person . . . themselves! . . . and was able to stress that life is more interesting if their constant companion is a well-informed and interesting person."

HARRIETTE S. ABELS
Author and Teacher
Writing the Category Novel
Writing for Children & Young Adults

"I was happy to share my love of history with the students. I enjoyed their excitement and enthusiasm for the subject."

PAUL DENUBILO
First Company of Richmond
Howitzers, Confederate Artillery Group
Civil War Re-Enactor

"My participation as a newspaper editor interacting with all those bright, enthusiastic young students was a terrific boost. I was amazed, yet greatly heartened, to see the intelligence, interest and responsiveness among these representatives of a generation that too many have already written off. The Guest Readers Program reinforces the efforts put forth by the teaching professionals and underscores the importance of parent involvement in a young America's total education experience."

RON LATIMORE
Former Editor of The Acorn

"As a school psychologist, one of my fondest memories was participating in the Guest Readers Program. I was energized by the students' responses and attention during the story and discussion. I will always cherish the letters I received after my visit."

ELAINE MASSION
School Psychologist
Los Angeles Unified School District

"It was a wonderful experience to read to the students. Everyone should participate!"

CATHIE WRIGHT
California State Senator, 19th District

"The Guest Readers Program was a wonderful opportunity. The benefits were mutual. Most children do not know what a dietitian is unless, unfortunately, they are ill and in the hospital. With my presentation, the students learned about my job and about good nutrition. It was a valuable experience for me because I could participate in a community service. The Guest Readers Program was positive for both me and the children."

CARYN J. YARNELL, M.S., R.D.
Dietitian

"Six members of the Society for Creative Anachronism (a nonprofit international education organization that re-creates the Middle Ages and early Renaissance) used the book as a springboard to describe some of the things we have learned about the Middle Ages and what we do, such as singing, dancing, cooking, armoring/fighting, and the concepts of chivalry and honor. Reading the book was an excellent way for us to segue into the information we usually teach in school demonstrations, which is one of SCA's purposes."

DAYLE A. DERMATIS
(a.k.a. Lady Rhieinwen Cyfarwydd ferch Angarad)
Middle Ages Re-Enactor

APPENDIX

Sample Materials to Use for Arranging Guest Readers' Appearances

SAMPLE SCHOOL NEWSLETTER AD

WANTED

GUEST READERS FOR [grade] CLASSES

Are you a lion tamer? Can you yodel?
Do you collect dinosaur bones?
Whatever your occupation talent or hobby,
we invite you to share your specialty by reading a related book.
(We will provide the book!)
For further information, contact [coordinator's name and tele-
phone number].

Sample Letter to Parents

(Date)

Dear Parents,

We invite you to participate in [school's name]'s Guest Readers Program and to visit our [grade] classes to read a story related to your job or hobby and then to describe your work/hobby. (We will provide the book for you to read!) This exciting program expands the students' view of the world while promoting the idea that reading is fun for everyone.

If you have an interesting occupation or special talent/hobby to share with our students, please contact [coordinator's name and telephone number] or please return the form below to your child's teacher [or the school office]. If you have a friend or family member who would like to be a Guest Reader, please let us know.

Thank you,

[Coordinator's name or School Principal's name]

GUEST READERS PROGRAM

(Please print)

Your name and phone number_____

_____

Child's name _____

Your relationship to child (parent, friend, etc.)_____

Teacher's name and room number_____

Occupation, hobby, talent, special interest _____

_____

No. 1 Sample Letter to Potential Guest Reader

[Type the letter on school stationery. Always follow up letters with a telephone call.]

[Date]

[Guest Reader's name]
[Guest Reader's address]

Dear [Guest Reader's name],

It would be our pleasure to have you participate in the Guest Readers Program that I am coordinating at [name of school].

Community members are asked to read a story related to their jobs or hobbies and then to briefly describe their work or specialty. (We provide the book!) When appropriate, a demonstration is given. In this way, we hope to motivate children to read and also to educate them about careers and other areas of interest. Volunteer readers have already included [list Guest Readers, such as an actor, a chemist, etc.].

We hope you will accept our invitation and will be able to find some time in [month] to visit our [grade] classes. We will be happy to accommodate your schedule.

I look forward to hearing from you, at which time we can discuss the details.

Sincerely,

[Coordinator's name]
[Coordinator's address—optional]
[Coordinator's telephone number]

No. 2 Sample Letter to Potential Guest Reader

[Type the letter on school stationery. Always follow up letters with a telephone call.]

[Date]

[Guest Reader's name]
[Guest Reader's address]

Dear [Speakers Bureau Coordinator's name],

We would appreciate it if you could arrange for a [position, such as basketball player] to participate in the Guest Readers Program that I am coordinating for [grade] classes at [name of school].

The Guest Readers Program invites members of the community to read books related to their professions or hobbies and to briefly talk about their work or specialty. (We will provide the book!)

Several dates we would like to suggest as possibilities are [dates] at [times]. The appearance should take no longer than [time frame].

We are excited about the prospect of a [position, such as basketball player] visiting our school and hope it can be scheduled.

We look forward to hearing from you.

Sincerely,

[Coordinator's name]
[Coordinator's address—optional]
[Coordinator's phone number]

TELEPHONE SCRIPT

1. Ask for the community relations or public relations department. If one does not exist, ask to talk to someone who can arrange for a speaker to visit the school.

2. When you reach the appropriate party say:

"Hello. My name is [coordinator's name], and I am the coordinator of the Guest Readers Program for the [grade] at [name of school] in [name of town]."

"The Guest Readers Program asks people from the community to read books to the children about their jobs and then to briefly talk about their work."

"We would like to invite you to visit our school to be a Guest Reader."

"In the past, we have had [list Guest Readers, such as an actor, chemist, etc.] volunteer to read to our students."

"We hope you can find time to participate in this worthwhile program. We will provide the book so you don't have to worry about finding one! And we will be happy to accommodate your schedule."

3. If the contact is not interested, ask for a referral to someone else in the field. If the contact is interested, see "Preparing the Guest Reader" in the first chapter, "Getting It Together," for additional information.

SAMPLE CONFIRMATION LETTER

[Type the letter on school stationery. Always follow up letters with a telephone call.]

April 30, 1997

Ms. Jan Smith
55 Fifth Street
Any City, CA 9——

Dear Ms. Smith,

We are very excited about your visit to our school on Friday, May 17, 1997! The classes are currently studying European Middle Ages so your presentation is especially timely.

Enclosed is an information sheet, a map to the school, a letter giving permission to bring historic weaponry onto campus, a copy of the read-aloud book, and "Hints for Reading Aloud," which I send to all Guest Readers. On the information sheet, I list a "Suggested Introduction to the Book," "Possible Discussion Topics" and "Suggested Demonstration." Please know that these are only suggestions. I realize you have an established presentation.

If you have any questions, do not hesitate to call me. I look forward to meeting you. Again, many thanks to you and your colleagues for volunteering your time.

Sincerely,

Jane Doe
Guest Readers Program Coordinator
(555) 555-5555

Sample Information Sheet

[This accompanies the confirmation letter. Try to fit the information on one page.]

INFORMATION SHEET FOR THE GUEST READER

Guest Reader   Jan Smith and members of SCA—(555) 555-0000

Topic   Middle Ages

Date   Friday, May 17, 1997

Time   9:30 AM–approx. 12:00 PM (We will meet in the school lobby at 9:30 AM for set-up. The custodian will be on hand to help.)

Location   Anytown Middle School 55 Main St. (555) 000-0000. Take Rte # 00. Exit Main Street (East). Map enclosed.

Presentation Schedule   10:00 AM–11:00 AM—Group I (two 7th grade classes)
11:00 AM–12:00 PM—Group II (two 7th grade classes)
(I will escort you to each group's classroom.)

Audience   There are approx. 120 students, 60 in each group. They are 12–13 years old.

Book   *Sir Gawain and the Loathly Damsel,* retold and illustrated by Joanna Troughton. It takes approx. 6 minutes to read.

Suggested Introduction of Book   Knights were very important to the society of the Middle Ages. You have heard of the great King Arthur and the Knights of the Round Table. This story, written and illustrated by Joanna Troughton, is adapted from a fifteenth-century poem about one of Arthur's best-loved knights, Sir Gawain.

Possible Discussion Topics   • Give a brief overview of the history of the Middle Ages. [A detailed outline appears in "Discussion Topics" in "Program Plan V" if you wish to use it.] • Briefly explain feudal society, chivalry, everyday life in a castle and village, including the role of women and children, marriage, education, religion, medicine, food, work and leisure pastimes.

Suggested Demonstrations   • Demonstrate crafts, such as carding and spinning wool into yarn. • Play musical instruments and sing songs from the time period. • Describe your clothing and armor. (Pass around a knight's helmet so the students can feel how heavy it is.)
• Engage in mock combat.

HINTS FOR READING ALOUD

1. Allow the audience a few minutes to settle down before you begin.

2. Include in the introduction of the book, the title, name of author and illustrator.

3. Make sure the audience can see the illustrations. If possible, show the pictures to the audience while you are reading the text. Hold the book in one hand, slightly to the side of your head, away from and in front of your body. This technique takes practice. If you feel uncomfortable please first read the text on the page and then show the picture to the class. If there are illustrations on adjoining pages, please read the text on both pages before showing the pictures. With a large group, you will have to "pan" or show the pictures from one side of the audience to the other.

4. Use plenty of expression when reading. Try to change the tone and pitch of your voice for different characters. Stress important words. Make certain words come to life. For example, if the word is "tired," sound tired.

5. Read at a natural pace—not too fast or too slowly. However, adjust the pace of the reading to fit the story or to set a mood. For example, read a suspenseful part slowly, drawing out the words.

6. If the students ask questions during the reading, answer patiently and then continue reading. If there are constant interruptions, say that you will answer questions after the story.

7. Review the book in advance for any parts you may want to eliminate or elaborate on. Please practice reading aloud.

8. Please practice giving the presentation. Be aware of timing, expressiveness and clarity of explanations. Remember to maintain eye contact with the entire group, not just the children directly in front of you.

9. Most important, have fun! Your enthusiasm will be contagious.

SAMPLE SCHEDULE

[Give copies to the principal, teachers, school office, and keep one for yourself.]

GUEST READER'S SCHEDULE

Guest Reader: Jan Smith and members of the Society for Creative Anachronism

Topic: Middle Ages

Date: Friday, May 17, 1997

Schedule: 10:00 AM–11:00 AM—Mrs. Brown/Mrs. Gold
(Location: Room 10)

11:00 AM–12:00 PM—Mrs. Silver/Mr. Gray
(Location: Room 12)

Deadline for thank-you notes: Wednesday, May 22, 1997.
Please place them in my box in the office. Thank you!

[If the presentation is to be held at one location, use *Location* as a separate heading. If there is to be only one presentation, use the heading *Time* instead of *Schedule.* See the example below.]

GUEST READER'S SCHEDULE

Guest Reader: Jan Smith and members of the Society for Creative Anachronism

Topic: Middle Ages

Date: Friday, May 17, 1997

Time: 10:00 AM–11:00 AM

Location: Library

Deadline for thank-you notes: Wednesday, May 22, 1997.
Please place them in my box in the office. Thank you!

SAMPLE THANK-YOU LETTER

[Type on school stationery.]

May 22, 1997

Ms. Jan Smith
55 Fifth Street
Any City, CA 9———

Dear Ms. Smith,

Many thanks to you and your colleagues for an enjoyable and informative presentation! You made history come to life!

As you can see from the students' letters, you have inspired them to learn more about the Medieval era. You have enriched their education and provided them with an exciting experience I'm sure they will not forget.

Again, thank you for being so generous with your time and your talents.

My best,

Jane Doe
Guest Readers Program Coordinator

SAMPLE UPDATE LETTER TO PARENTS

[Type on school stationery.]

[Date]

Dear Parents,

In the beginning of the school year, a Guest Readers Program was established at [name of school]. People from the community and [name of school] parents were invited to read stories connected to their jobs or hobbies and to briefly describe their specialty. The goal of the program is to help expand the students' view of the world as well as to motivate young people to read.

Many thanks go to all the Guest Readers who have shared their time thus far and to [list names of teachers and principal] for their support.

Below is a list of Guest Readers and books that have been presented this past semester. Also included are related books. If you are interested, ask the teacher for a more complete bibliography.

Please encourage your child to visit the library to borrow one or more of these books and to "read more about it."

Sincerely,

[Coordinator's name]

Suggested format of the list:
Title of book and author
Related books (list only a few)
Guest Reader's name and title
Date of Guest Reader's visit

SAMPLE PRESS RELEASE

[Some organizations have special stationery to be used for press releases. If this is not available, use the library's regular business stationery with letterhead. The text of the press release is usually double-spaced.]

For Further Information Contact: FOR IMMEDIATE RELEASE
Jane Doe
(555)555-5555

MEMBERS OF THE SOCIETY FOR CREATIVE ANACHRO-NISM WILL BE GUEST READERS AT ANY CITY LIBRARY

Any City, CA—Members of the Society for Creative Anachronism, a nonprofit educational organization that recreates the Middle Ages, will be Guest Readers at Any City Library, 00 Oak Street, on Friday, May 17, 1997 at 10:00 AM.

Jan Smith, also known as Lady Madeleine, will read *Sir Gawain and the Loathly Damsel,* a legend based on a fifteenth-century poem retold and illustrated by Joanna Troughton. Wearing period costumes, the group will talk about life during the Medieval era and will demonstrate crafts, perform music and engage in mock combat. Although the program is primarily geared to young people in grades 3 to 8, everyone is welcome to attend.

The library's Guest Readers Program invites community members to read a story related to their job or special interest and then to briefly describe their work. The goal is to broaden children's view of the world as well as to promote the idea that books are fun for everyone.

Index

About the Author

ADRIENNE WIGDORTZ ANDERSON has an MA (UCLA) with a specialty in children's theatre, and a BA (Rutgers University) in theatre arts and education. She produced a National Public Radio special, *Seniors and the Arts,* and was co-producer of the award-winning children's television show, *Rainy Days.* She was also an associate producer of the children's special, *Way to Go,* and the producer of the children's theatre group, *The Salt Water Taffy Players.* As a puppeteer, she appeared with *Bob Baker Marionette Theatre, The Puppetworks, The Muppet Movie,* and in commercials. She currently presents a one-woman show for children entitled *Bedtime Stories.*

She has extensive experience as a creative dramatics specialist with elementary schools, and presently teaches creative movement to preschool students. In addition, she is a freelance writer and has published articles in many publications.

Anderson created and introduced the Guest Readers Program at a preschool, and later coordinated the program at an elementary school and two middle schools. She received several awards for these efforts, including a Certificate of Appreciation from the City of Los Angeles, the NVJCC Edward Lieberman Guest Reader Program Award, and the Service Above Self Award from the Rotary Club.

Her first book, *Firefighter—Read Me a Book!,* explains how to organize the Guest Readers Program for preschool and lower elementary groups.